"Not everything that is faced can be changed, but nothing can be changed until it is faced."

James Baldwin

Author's Note

Argument is a pejorative term. I do not wish to argue with you, the reader, about issues in this book. I do not want to draw lines that place you on one side and me on the other. I do not wish to try and persuade you that I am right and that you are wrong.

However, many individuals from the public, the employees whom I supervised, other elected officials with whom I worked and interacted, the members of the press corps, party leaders, and party members from both sides of the aisle have at times crossed the line of *common decency*. No longer was it just politics, but rather the attacks were getting quite personal with the goal of maligning my professional reputation, undermining the integrity of my friends and allies, and maliciously hurting my family.

You individuals who trafficked in these kinds of personal attacks lacked integrity and character. In fact, persons such as you who consciously lied, misstated the facts, misled others, committed perjury in order to garner financial rewards and simply displayed ignorance to*wards* so many others who were never deserving of your mean-spirited behavior are in a word, reprehensible.

Rather than being useful as a member of the community or as an employee or as an elected political figure, you chose to be useless in dispensing your obligations as a person in a civilized society or as a person in service to the public. No, you chose uselessness, serving only yourself and in many cases, serving your political cronies, who used you as a puppet.

By your behavior you have exposed your prevaricating selves. It is now time for me to peel away your façade so that others can see the pretentious you. After all, we must all stand responsible for our actions. Often times we do so by standing tall, with humility, on our own two feet, no matter how harsh the result. For others, unfortunately, it takes some one else to call them out!

DEDICATION

This book is affectionately and respectfully dedicated to my loving family, supportive friends and loyal constituents who have stood by me throughout my many years of successful public service. Regardless of the circumstances, these wonderful people continue to believe in me. They do so unconditionally because they know who I am, not as defined by my adversaries, who have confused the image with the reality, but rather they see me as the person who I really am as demonstrated through my public and private actions.

I could never quantify the quality and intensity of this belief but suffice it to say, I humbly accept it. This commitment from these wonderful people speaks volumes as to their character and integrity. Those of whom I speak know who you are. I would surely do a disservice to someone if I were to begin mentioning names and regrettably forget someone. That truly would be unforgivable. We have walked many a road together on this long journey and we have succeeded where others have failed and will continue to fail. You who fail will do so because you lack the spirit, integrity, conviction and loyalty that we gave towards every mission and project that we undertook as a team. We have left a legacy, one that can be never undone no matter how hard the purveyors of doom and gloom try. The *sad sacks* will never measure up to the standard that we have set. They just don't get it! They lack the ability, competence and integrity to walk our walk. They are absent of honor, loyalty and conviction.

As we reflect upon our service to the people, we do so by holding our heads high with pride. We have made all the difference in building a Premier Community. And for those of you who are truly honest with yourself, I do believe that you too will never forget our contributions. I am confident that time and history will treat us kindly.

Speaking Out and Up

The First Amendment guarantees every American the right to freedom of speech. It is the one right that defines America apart from any other nation. Americans fought and died in defense of this right. Attacks on the First Amendment have come from all corners of this free society, but have been successfully deterred. Even when the judicial system has failed to act prudently and responsibly in defining the tenets of free speech and the free press in its many forms, the people of this great nation have stood tall, unified in one voice in expressing their discontentment which was heard loudly and clearly by the courts and our elected representatives.

That is not to say that at times, there is an abuse of the First Amendment. I am quite sure that each one of us could point to one or more instances when we feel that individuals have once again, stepped over that line of decency hiding behind the First Amendment. As it may be, this is neither the time, place nor forum for such a discussion. On that very same subject, however, I will invoke my constitutional right to the First Amendment in expressing my views in this book. However, in doing so, I will apply several "Golden Rules" that will guide me in my writing. These Golden Rules are the very same ones that I used in dispensing the duties of my office and in the manner that I addressed the people with whom I came in contact. I have always believed that these Golden Rules provide an excellent set of checks and balances as related to one's sense of honesty, sincerity and fair play.

Many of these Golden Rules that I have lived by throughout my life can be attributed to Eleanor Roosevelt.

The Golden Rules

- Many people will walk in and out of your life, but only true friends will leave footprints on your life.

- To handle yourself use your head; to handle others, use your heart.

- If someone betrays you once, it is his/her fault; it she/he betrays you again, it is your fault.

- Great minds discuss ideas; average minds discuss events; small minds discuss people.

- He who loses money loses much; he who loses a friend, loses much more; he who loses faith, loses all.

- Beautiful people are accidents of nature, but beautiful old people are works of art.

- Learn from the mistakes of others. You can't live long enough to make all of them yourself

- See challenges as opportunities and adversity as a blessing.

- Give results, not excuses.

- If it doesn't kill you, it is bound to make you stronger.

- It is not so much what you say, but rather how you say it.

- Empty heads, like empty barrels, make the most noise.

- Never trust a person who has someone else sign his letters to the editor, especially the ugly ones.

- If you are not the lead dog, the scenery never changes.

- Why is it that I could never be a confidential unnamed source for a newspaper reporter?

- An elected official who has "no comment" usually hasn't a clue.

- People who practice religion every day of their lives are in better shape then those who practice only once a week for an hour or two.

- Life is very much like a play inasmuch as once the curtain goes up, it doesn't come down until the final scene. This life is not a rehearsal, so live it to the fullest!

INTRODUCTION

Why do people write books? A good friend of mine provided me with the following reason and I have embraced it: One writes a book because one has thoughts, ideas, feelings and experiences that he feels compelled to record for himself and for others to share.

This chronicle of my public service to Washington Township, N.J. will span about 25 years or so. Not all events will be written about! Rather, I will carefully highlight what I believe to be significant events, occurrences, people, places, activities and issues that have had a cogent impact on the community, the residents, the employees, my friends and of course, myself. This chronicle will reach beyond the community that I served and touch county, and state elected officials, appointed officials, residents and the press that affected the community and its leaders in both a negative and positive fashion.

I am sure that many individuals will not be pleased with my characterization of them. But then again, it is my personal opinion, my perception of who they really are. Not the image mind you, but rather the reality. To many who read this book, you will have lived this entire adventure with me and therefore so much more will be familiar. Others may not be able to identify or relate to individual names or events. And some will find that much of what I have written is without significance. Although that may be the case, I would ask that those readers look at the actions of certain individuals and the consequences of their actions predicated on the reader's understanding and sense of fair play, honesty and good judgment. In fact, your objectivity will be a welcome breath of fresh air to me, having lived with all these thoughts for so very long.

I would be less than honest if I tried to lead the reader to the conclusion that my motives in writing this book are solely altruistic. Not hardly! Being a proud man who gave of his time and talent to my community, I do want to ensure, to the degree possible, that my contributions are remembered. Given the lack of character found in so many who have been elected to public office in the last several years, it is obvious that they will do just about anything to diminish the quality, depth and scope of my administration's contributions to the community. Perhaps by re-writing history and taking credit for themselves by renaming everything they can in honor of deceased members of their political party, they can, in their own minds, justify all their actions. In over two decades of public service I have come to the realization that the vast majority of politicians are not creative, imaginative or innovative. However, to their credit, they do know a good thing when they see it and will do whatever it takes to get on that bandwagon pronto. Too bad the inquiring eye of the press doesn't see this and write articles that expose these charlatans.

I can also understand that many readers may think me arrogant for standing tall and laying claim to my accomplishments that have been achieved through hard work, dedication and commitment. To you I answer, "Not arrogance, but pride." Considering what my adversaries have tried to blame on me over the years, I have earned my stripes and paid my dues, which I believe entitles me to state my contributions to the community without fear of criticism. I am sufficiently astute to evaluate my contributions to the community in terms of enhancing and improving the quality of life for the overwhelming majority of people I represented. I am also aware that many individuals will chide me by stating that this book is nothing more than my personal recollections, perceptions and opinions. Although that latter statement may have some validity, let me assure the reader that I have voluminous files consisting of tapes, letters and memos that will support ALL my claims.

In my travels as an educator, mayor and state legislator, I have come to the conclusion that communities throughout the region, state and even the nation are more similar than not. Neighborhood concerns transcend the boundaries of race, color, religion and financial station. Basically, people living in suburbia, USA, want the same things. Other elected officials, no matter who and where you are, can draw some parallels from my vast experiences, especially at the local level where politics is the most difficult. Perhaps you won't be motivated to write a book, but I do encourage you to at least keep a journal for your own edification. Memories are made of experiences, both good and bad!

Given my years of service in the public arena, I was enough of a realist to accept that I could make friends and enlist enemies. It is impossible to have the kinds of successes enjoyed during my administration without creating change. And as many of you know making change does not come without a price! Basically, change will rub people who want the status quo the wrong way. These bastions of obtuse thinking perceive change as an assault on what is comfortable and secure. Generally, change will shift the center of power away from those who hold the reins of a community into new and more capable and creative hands. When all this change begins to develop, you can be damn sure that there will be a contingency of people who will do everything and anything to stop you by orchestrating subversive plans that would shock even the most seasoned political figure. You may ask why anyone would take the time and energy to do this. Well the answer is a simple one. These kinds of people are short-range thinkers—uncreative and severely lacking in the innovations department. They respond to their initial knee-jerk instinct and that is generally being negative towards anything that they did not think about. Of course, given their limited thinking, you can anticipate a negative response to just about anything. These little people feel threatened—fearful of losing control of their little empires. They will never embrace change, no matter how often they are proved wrong. They are vengeful and jealous, fearful of accepting progressive and creative ideas simply because they do not understand. They would rather be a stumbling block in the way of a community's progress than admit that they are wrong. Now that is truly a sad commentary on some elected and appointed officials, employees and, yes, some residents too.

People who live in the subculture of doom and gloom do not go away easily. Like the poor, they will always be with us. Their weapon of personal choice is attacks, replete with rumors, lies, innuendo, distortions and a cadre of other subversive and manipulative aspersions. Either they fail to see how they hurt others or they choose not to see and they enjoy the havoc they create. I'm sure that most people would agree that this is a twisted sense of morality and values.

Another compelling reason for writing a book is to correct, for the record, the misinformation and sensationalism perpetrated upon the public by the members of the press. Over the years, I have come to realize that the press operates without boundaries. Too often reporters and editors deal with the lives of people as though they were objects. The human factor is all but ignored. Reporters begin to write fiction, not facts, and we then see editors who are quick to judge by making unfair criticisms of issues of which they have little or no knowledge, based only upon that reporter's story. Of course, to compound the problem, reporters and editors are slow, if ever, to apologize for their ignorant and arrogant remarks. There is no question in my mind that the major abuses of the First Amendment come from the members of the press corps. You have read as well as I the scandals that have infiltrated even the most prestigious newspapers in this country. Apparently anything goes to get a story, and it happens right here in our own backyard. Too often reporters are easy marks for the members of the public or disgruntled employees who traffic in rumors and gossip. Reporters love to deal with "confidential sources" who, for the most part, are politicians or political wannabes. The facts need to be reported, but the story must be honest, accurate, fair, balanced and reflect parity to all those involved. In our neck of the woods, this is not the motto of most reporters and their editors. Taking a hard look at my years of service, I'd say that I have found only five reporters that I would consider journalists. The rest of them are just your everyday runts-of-the-litter reporters and editors!

And finally, it is essential for me to point out to the reader that the administration that I headed *NEVER* had a scandal. Of course there were rough times, accusations, innuendos and the like. But through all the political lies and the rhetoric spewed forth from the mouths of the spiteful, there was never one investigation by any agency that substantiated any improper conduct! To the shame of the community, many of these scurrilous individuals are still around. It appears, at least for the present, that many of those individuals were rewarded for their part in the character assassination.

I trust that this introduction has provided a thumbnail sketch of what this book will focus on. No matter what many may say about this book, be assured that I am not writing it for the purpose of retribution. That is seemingly taking care of itself as more and more of my adversaries are shooting themselves in the foot. I am simply setting the record straight. I am attempting to repair the damage to my reputation and the reputation of others unfairly attacked simply because of their loyalty and support of me. I am also attempting to demonstrate the hurt that can be manifested by the reckless and irresponsible actions of a few individuals whose blatant disregard for honesty and accuracy can cause irreversible pain to many. It is now time to level the playing field!

And finally, it is important to note that I mean no disrespect to the people I have written about who have died, or to their families who live with their memories. However, there is no way that I can ignore how they interfaced with me while they were alive. I believe that it is important to remind ourselves that we will be remembered and that we will be judged by the way we lived our life, and not how we died.

CONTENTS

PART I

PART II

**THE ARDUOUS TIMES—THROUGH
ADVERSITY WE CREATE OPPORTUNITIES** 101

Part I

The Prelude

Chapter 1

COMMUNITY PROFILE AND A BRIEF HISTORY

To really understand my community, it is essential to provide an overview of how Washington Township emerged from a sleeping New Jersey farming community of 23 square miles, absent of all public services, into Gloucester County's largest municipality, rich in votes, tax dollars, resources, public and private services, education, commercial, industrial and professional businesses and diverse residential neighborhoods of such a nature as not to be found anywhere else in Gloucester County. (I caution the reader at this point that if you are looking for the romantic and sugar-coated history of Washington Township from its birth to the present day, I suggest that you visit the Township's library, located in the Hollydell Corporate Park.) As with most farm communities throughout New Jersey, and probably throughout this nation, we are always sure to find the local town historian who makes every attempt to remind people about the roots of their community. In today's mobile society, most people do not have deep roots in a particular community. Today we find families choosing to direct their concern and interest to their own family's roots which, for many Township families, lie on the other side of the Delaware River, the USA or even the Atlantic and Pacific Oceans. In Washington Township that is most assuredly the case. Given the growth of this Township over the past 50 years, only a handful of people can call themselves "pioneers."

Many years ago, perhaps in the late 19th or early 20th century, several farmers met in a kitchen of one of the many farmhouses that dotted the landscape. Or perhaps these hearty farmers took the time to meet at the local tavern to discuss politics and business over a few beers. Regardless of the setting, their mission was to discuss the incorporating of some 23 square miles of beautiful, rich farmland and lush forest that provided a home to fowl and animals with pristine lakes and waterways that supported an abundance of marine life.

Although historical accounts vary, depending on who is telling the story, small hamlets dotted the area with the names Bunker Hill, Chapel Heights, Turnersville, Cross Keys, Hurffville, Grenloch, Chestnut Ridge, Orchard Valley and Nob Hill. Many of these names really define large farms as opposed to actual communities. (I am sure that a few names have been omitted but that will not change the eventual transformation that was to take place.) These early settlers and landowners realized that incorporation would unite these parcels, increasing their value, providing the legal basis to create a municipality and to define the disputed boundaries separating Gloucester County and Camden County. Excepting Nob Hill, which is separated by Camden County's Lakeland Facility, all other properties to be included in the merger and subsequent incorporation were contiguous. Considering that these men were good Christian men, they looked to a nation's hero for a name. Washington Township was born!

Urban legend tends to paint a very kind and romantic picture of the Township's forefathers. Without stepping on the toes of their descendants, it doesn't take a scholar to reach the conclusion that these early settlers did indeed make several grievous errors in planning that would come to haunt this Township well into the 21st century. Even more grievous was the failure of subsequent town leaders in the period from 1930 to 1970 to see what was needed to provide an orderly creation of a well-planned community. Again, this lack of vision early in the Township's development would only exacerbate and compound the problems that would haunt all future town leaders, and thus becoming the rallying point for the residents and the gadflies of this community.

It wouldn't have taken much for the early leaders of this community to see what other towns and cities were doing. A little research and objective thinking would have well rewarded future residents of Washington Township. Sometimes we don't know all the answers and we need to look beyond our parochial borders for answers. In the development of Philadelphia, New York City, Washington, D.C. and the grand City of Camden (prior to its demise, circa 1960), a Master Plan was used. And there were smaller residential communities such as Woodbury, Clayton, Pitman, Swedesboro, Williamstown and the City of Vineland that relied on organized development that was tied to a Master Plan. In Camden County, model communities such as Haddonfield and Collingswood set outstanding examples of careful planning that incorporated the most basic of ideas, such as a town center and connecting sidewalks. Simply, a *long-range* Master Plan needs to be developed in order to provide an overall blueprint of the entire community, even if many of those creative and innovative ideas seem to be unrealistic at the time of conception and may, in fact, never reach fruition. Those communities and cities embracing that kind of thinking were generally successful in their development The persons that commit to that kind of master planning have the right to be called *visionary thinkers and leaders.*

Regrettably the selling of land, parcel by parcel, with no Master Plan in a community's formative years, precludes the opportunity to interface that individual parcel of properties with one another, thus offsetting service-intense residential growth with tax-rich commercial and light industrial zoning. This critical mistake began a series of events that would lead to many problems as the Township emerged from the post-World War II era and the expansion of Route 42 and the building of the Walt Whitman Bridge. The unscrupulous land developers with their big ideas and well-paid lawyers were just waiting to move in and to take over. The local gentry was no match for the likes of these fast talkers, get-rich developers who operated under many corporate names, making many promises and commitments, of which very few were honored.

Chapter 2

HISTORICAL PERSPECTIVE

Washington Township's farms provided much in the way of fruits and vegetables to area restaurants, small and large grocery stores and course, the Campbell Soup Company. For many years, trucks loaded to capacity started early to ensure a place in the long lines that were part of everyday business at Campbell Soup in the City of Camden. Many a high school boy found work during the spring, summer and fall, planting and harvesting crops, as well as loading trucks.

After the end of World War II, there began a booming economical revitalization necessary to support the infusion of GI's into civilian life. Their lives had been interrupted to fight a war on foreign soil and now they were returning home and they too wanted to claim their part of the American Dream. Upon returning from the war, many boys who had left the farms to defend a nation decided that farming was not for them and they sought other types of employment or they took advantage of the GI College Bill. New Jersey's State Teachers Colleges at Glassboro, Trenton, Jersey City and Newark saw incredible growth during this period and needed to adjust curriculum, housing and staff to meet the demands of the new students who were older and more mature. Times were changing!

In the 1950's the farming industry had begun to see better days. Prices were dropping, larger farms were able to outproduce smaller farms, selling at lower and more competitive prices. Farm cooperatives were formed and the food industry that relied on the farmer for its products began to buy the farms and produce its own raw foods. Areas of the country with more favorable climates could produce year-round crops. With the expansion of trucking, air shipments, cold storage and frozen foods, the prices of wholesale farm products was affected and controlled by a market totally foreign to the local farmer. The era of the local farmer living off his land were numbered!

The landscape of South Jersey also began to change with the post-war housing building boom. Many of these returning veterans began to marry and start families of their own. Now they too wanted a new home and the United States Government cooperated by providing Veteran's Administration Housing Loans (VA mortgages). The building boom was underway and the vacant parcels of land in all the established communities gave way to new home construction. In many communities, the built-out level was reached very quickly. A crossroads had been reached!

More housing was needed. The planned communities called Levittowns on Long Island and in Pennsylvania became a model for other builders and established a barometer as to what Americans would accept relative to housing and the concept of tract housing. Pre-manufactured homes with much of the framing materials pre-cut to specific sizes, etc., shortened the time to complete a home and that put a roof over many a family's head in less than a 90 days. Given the low down payment and low interest rate, one could safely say that "Mr. Levitt came up with an award winning idea." Although the end result was cookie-cutter homes on farm land with little or no landscaping and neighborhoods that all looked the same, they were affordable homes in a good neighborhood that provided schools and local shopping for all its residents. Many sociologists declare this period the *advent of suburbia!*

With the completion of the Walt Whitman Bridge between Philadelphia and New Jersey and the desire of many young marrieds to flee the crowded and predominantly ethnic neighborhoods of South Philadelphia in exchange for a piece of the American Dream that included a single-family home on a parcel of property with a lawn, the eyes of the developers turned south to Gloucester Township (Camden County) and farm-rich Washington Township (Gloucester County) for possible building sites. Did anyone in 1950 ever think that this building boom would span some 50 years?

Farmland that had been in families for generations now took on a whole new value as developers quietly began to take options on farm after farm in sleepy Washington Township. Imagine that you are a farmer and every month you are getting a check from a developer as he goes through the process of getting approvals to build homes. It could be months or years before that developer gets approvals and during all that time you continue to get a check and you have the right to farm and to make whatever income you can. Now that is a good deal!

Imagine the farmer's delight when developers talked thousands of dollars not hundreds of dollars per acre? The farmers had found their retirement nest egg—a dream come true and rightfully so. It was their land and America is a capitalistic country. Good old Washington Township farmers were going to cash in on their piece of the American Dream. At first blush that seems to pass muster, but under the microscope we find that many of these farmers also sat on the Township Committee, the Planning Board or the Zoning Board. These officials were vested property owners and could ensure that their deal was the best and the most lucrative for their own family pocketbooks. Regrettably however, these hardworking and basically honest men of the fields were not prepared for the fast-talking developers, their lawyers or their planners who could make every housing development picture perfect. As history would prove, the picture was the only thing that was perfect.

Many hard and difficult lessons would be learned by the Township's elected and appointed officials for moving too quickly without proper guidance absent of sound and objective professional input. In some cases, the professional input expected from Township lawyers, engineers and planners was tainted since these so-called *trusted professionals* were silent partners in many of the projects, setting aside any personal or professional ethics in order to line their own pockets. To compound this period of what could be perceived as unethical conduct was the fact that many Township officials who had private businesses were hired as private contractors for the very same developers whose projects they voted on. It seemed that no one cared and I suppose these individuals thought who would ever know? From the image romanticizing that has occurred through the years about these individuals, these people were right: *no one did care!*

Chapter 3

EARLY MISTAKES
REVISITED

Though Washington Township grew and changed without a Master Plan, for years, even through my administration, elected officials and residents used the Master Plan phrase, hoping that somehow or other it could solve whatever problem or issue was, for the moment, on the front burner of the political stove. *The truth of the matter is that the Master Plan is a working document—a current and future plan in transition that needs to be reviewed regularly.* More than not, the uninformed and the misinformed would refer to the Master Plan as though it was sacred, the Holy Grail or the Ark of the Covenant. It was neither of these and in that misconception of the Master Plan, I will try to be as lucid as possible and as kind as possible in explaining the mistakes of our leaders in the period 1930-1980. I don't want to offend those individuals that time, or their death or the re-invent-ing of themselves has made them an urban legend. *"This above all: to thine own self be true."*

So, let us enumerate the mistakes of those responsible for breathing life into Washington Township during the critical formative years:

- Early on in the development of this community, elected leaders failed to have a vision, projecting the 23 square miles as ONE integrated community.

- The focus was on selling parcels of land regardless of contiguousness prevailed for what appeared to be personal financial gain.

- They failed to employ a professional and creative planner who would design the entire 23 square miles, developing areas and parcels of land to provide services for the residential growth.

- They omitted proper planning that would develop zoning to incorporate appropriate transitional zones to insulate and buffer residential from non-residential development.

- They lacked an intense and productive interfacing with the State and the County in determining short- and long-range plans for primary and secondary roads, as well as mass-transportation venues.

- They did no future thinking regarding location of water wells, sanitary sewer lines and other public services including gas and electric, and updating the Master plan as new advances and techniques were developed.

- They had no awareness of the negative impact on the health of individuals by permitting the construction of septic wells and cesspools in the 20th century. [An examination of established communities could have provided guidelines for the Township.]

- They failed to plan and design a configuration of the community's layout, whether a hub-spoke or a grid design, therefore providing for a REAL town center or downtown area so very essential in creating community harmony and cohesiveness.

- There was no proper planning to enable various individual parcels of property to connect, either by sidewalks or green belts to avoid isolated residential development.

- They did not request studies of the impact residential growth would have on roadways and other traffic concerns due to the additional vehicles that would be used in residents traveling to work and shopping areas outside the community.

- They failed to develop a comprehensive plan to encourage commercial and industrial growth to support residential growth. The balance was disproportionate.

- In the early stages of development, they failed to set up with the United States Postal Service ONE central post office to serve the entire community. With a complete

Master Plan, although much of the design would be fu-
turistic thinking, it would have been obvious that this
community would surpass all others in South Jersey.
(Failure to do this has resulted in Washington Township
being served by seven post offices, with only two of the
mailing addresses actually a part of the community, those
being Turnersville and Grenloch. Other mailing addresses
include Sewell, Glassboro, Pitman, Blackwood,
Williamstown and Sicklerville none of which are part of
Washington Township.)

- They erred in creating an independent authority to provide required services in the area of water and sewer.
  These essential community services would have better
  served the residents more appropriately as a department
  of the municipal government that could exercise more
  control over development via the Planning Board and
  the Township Committee (later to become the Township
  Council.)

- They failed to provide adequate and substantial building line setbacks from county and state roads, a problem that would be revisited numerous times with frustration as the community developed. Expansion for the
  reasons of safety and convenience for the residents along
  the community's roadways would be precluded due to
  the fact that building lines were approved too close to
  the roads. This not only addressed roads, but sidewalks,
  something the Township was sorely lacking until 1990,
  when my administration changed all that.

Rather than enumerate any more glaring mistakes, I believe that it is abundantly clear that early leaders of this community failed to enlist the services of professionals with a vision who would have been able to provide invaluable input into the planning of a totally new community. Regrettably, they hired short-sighted individuals, lacking in creativity who could not think outside the box. A golden opportunity was lost!

The opportunity to create the ideal suburbia seemingly was not apparent to these men of limited vision. The opportunity to plan a community from Mother Earth does not present itself too often. This opportunity, lost or purposely ignored by the early leaders of Washington Township, would in the future become the basis for public outcries over many issues:

- Open space

- Overbuilding of residential units

- Zoning problems

- School busing

- Neighborhood discord

- Traffic problems

- Public services, including water restriction, lack of sanitary sewer and electrical service

- Parks and recreation

- Overcrowded schools

- Affordable housing

- Property taxes

Public meetings became soap boxes for the informed and sincere individuals who truly cared about solving problems by addressing the issues head on as objectively as possible. However, as all of us know, there are always those individuals whose sole reason for involvement in any issue is to create strife. Why these unfortunate, misguided and sometimes malevolent individuals got involved is really not a mystery, at least to me. They were usually ignorant of the facts or didn't care about facts. Why let the facts complicate your opinion on the subject? Or these sad people were politically motivated to do their best in blaming someone for the problem in the hope of building a platform for themselves or others in launching a political career. These people were legends in their own mind!

Whether genuine or disingenuous as to motives, single-issue or vested-interest individuals or groups that reflect this kind of thinking, miss the bigger picture by being so myopic. Going through life with blinders on is only good to train horses and does not serve people well. *The bigger picture means viewing the community as a whole and not just your piece of the American Dream.* You have no argument from me that democracy is based upon the principles of social equality and respect for individuals within a community. However, what individuals or a group of individuals seem to ignore or fail to comprehend is that the individual's right must, at times, acquiesce to what is best for the majority. Democracy is the rule of the majority, not the minority in most reasonable situations. Of course nothing is really ever etched in stone, so the response to the latter statement may be challenged by those statements:

- The squeaky wheel gets the oil.

- Isn't this an election year?

- Do you know how many votes we control?

- We'll take care of you at the polls.

- You haven't heard or seen the last of us.

Ah, the kind sentiments hurled at politicians from the public! Oh what the heck, it's only politics so don't take it personally. If you are talking to me or about me, *it is personal!*

Chapter 4

KEEPING GOVERNMENT ACCESSIBLE

N ew Jersey, like so many other states, provides its residents with a plethora of government models from which to choose in the operation of municipal and county government. In most cases, the people can decide through the ballot box how they wish to be governed. Surely this is democracy at work! Unfortunately, there are a few forms of government that should be removed from New Jersey's approved list, and I would urge the State Senate and Assembly to move forward on this matter. This action may not be politically correct or garner them votes or perhaps warrant an editorial on their innovative, creative and independent leadership. In fact, the only positive outcome of such an action will be that it will *benefit the people.* Imagine that—an action that has no residuals for the politicians! Knowing Trenton as I do, that will be a major feat to understand even by the most aggressive of lobbyists.

What I am addressing here are the forms of government that clearly defy all that is democratic by permitting elected officials the right to abdicate their duty of leadership to a non-elected employee. In this executive form of government, the elected body empowers an appointed individual to carry out the daily operations of government and all its related services. These County Executives or Business Administrators are quick to understand that their employment is directly tied to the coattails of the politicians who appointed them and not to the will of the people. Their loyalty is to the politicians. Such loyalty can be unhealthy, compromising the values and integrity of the most noble. After all folks, political jobs can come and go in the time it takes to count the ballots on election night. Such job *insecurity* can wreak havoc with the family and jeopardize severely the ability to obtain future employment in one's area of expertise. Therefore these appointed officials, who I hasten to add do *not* answer to the people, begin to build power bases within the framework of the government especially among and between the elected officials. They become a sort of "double agent." By the time these appointed officials or employees reach the double agent rung on the ladder of political debauchery, they have sold out as to their integrity, loyalty, morality and any degree of professionalism or self-respect that they once possessed. They may call what they do survival at any cost, but the public and the employees see them for what they really are—*unprincipled sellouts!*

At some point, the leaders in State government made the presumption that many elected officials had not the educational background, the intellectual capacity, or the ability (perhaps even lacked the interest) to assume the responsibility of running government on a day-to-day basis. Helping to validate that unproven presumption was the public. In most cases they believed that all elected officials should do their job with little or no compensation. Such a belief prevailed and struck a fear in many elected officials to even broach the subject of pay for services rendered lest they be the victim of reprisals from their constituents. It is ludicrous to think that anyone putting forth the time and energy in attempting to do their best in representing the people should not be compensated to some degree. Of course, the term *compensation* is relative and, depending on the breath, depth and scope of responsibilities and the functioning role of these elected officials in the government, a reasonable compensation can be established. There must be parameters established to define and limit free public service.

On the other side of the issue, many voters contend that the political system breeds mediocrity inasmuch as the candidates are recycled and the limitations of the two-party system don't really provide much in the choice of worthy candidates. Furthermore, many of those persons elected to public office are the not the brightest lights on the tree. With the only requirements to run for public office being residency and the ability to sign one's name, I suppose that in some communities we cannot expect too much in the way of leadership.

To circumvent the pay-for-services issue, many elected officials, sitting as a legislative body, began to authorize health benefits packages, mirroring what the employees were being provided. Considering the hours some elected officials give to their elected positions and the depth of their educational training and exceptional intellect and keen ability, the public is getting a bargain and shouldn't even raise an eyebrow if this matter becomes an issue by the press, uninformed members of the public or the political gadflies. Truly it is a non-issue and doesn't deserve the time to be discussed.

I am also quick to add without reservation that many elected officials are not deserving of any respectable compensation. These people elected into office are not leaders, lack any applicable skills, are unable to solve problems and are simply and totally inadequate. These are the politicians that open their mouths before engaging their brains and are numb when it comes to understanding the issues facing the community. No matter what they say or do, it reeks of politics. They are rightfully relegated to ribbon cuttings, local parades, showing up for community activities (no speeches please) or giving out resolutions or proclamations. For lack of a term that might summarize what they are good for, suffice to say we refer to them kindly as "ceremonial officials." In this capacity they really can do little or no harm. Now the public may ask, "Why would any town want officials like that?" Well, there is no intelligence test to qualify one to run for public office. If there were such a test, the field of candidates would be severely reduced to a few. No, the public makes the choice at the ballot box and unfortunately, all that glitters is not gold. The public needs to be much more discerning as to who should be elected to public office. Too often the voting public selects a candidate for all the wrong reasons or worse yet, can never get beyond political labels.

Today it is being said that voters have more choices of political candidates. If the voters choose wisely, they will elect competent leaders who can make a difference for a community. If these candidates fail to produce the anticipated results, then they need to be voted out of office at the next election. Of course that means that the public must be vigilant and determine for themselves as to what is happening in their community, county, state or nation. When it comes to evaluating if an elected official is doing his/her job, don't count on the advice of others and by all means, do not rely on the press to provide an accurate accounting. You must find out for yourself by attending meetings, talking to your representatives and by opening your eyes and seeing for yourself what is happening in your little part of the world.

It is incumbent upon the State of New Jersey and other states to revisit the statutes that provide the enabling legislation for the formation of government. Today more than ever, power must be taken out of the hands of appointed officials who answer only to the politicians. The people must have decision makers totally answerable to the electorate. Government is responsible to and must answer to the public. This idea of insulating decision makers from the public's view at any level is totally unacceptable. Today's public, whether they choose to exercise their right to vote, is nevertheless entitled to an open government with all access granted thereto. No one is above reproach and no one in government should be unapproachable. No exceptions please!

Chapter 5

WHY SHOULD I VOTE?

The society of the 21st century hasn't changed all that much from the society of the latter part of the 20th century. People in suburbia, USA, are pretty much doing the same thing. As a nation that was founded of the principles of freedom, I suppose it stands to reason that we have the right *not* to exercise those freedoms that have been provided us by so many who have gone before us. Still, I find it difficult to understand why so many Americans choose not to vote? I understand fully that the decision whether or not to vote rests in the hands of the individual. Not voting is a right, a freedom if you will. And like any other elected official, I have heard the reasons why people don't vote. As crafty as some of those reasons may seem they can all be reduced to one very simple phrase—*you just don't care!* To those who are not registered to vote, there is so very little anyone can say.

In the two-party system, which has pretty much dominated the country except in a few exceptions, the political
bosses prefer that not too many people vote. Surprised? Well,
you shouldn't be. Imagine a political system where the parties have a handle on those individuals who do vote to the
point of knowing that those votes will be there no matter
what. No matter who is on the ballot, the political gurus can
pretty much determine the number of votes that will be cast
for their candidate. In some areas of this state, the voter reg-
istration is so skewed towards one party that victory is almost certain no matter who the candidate may be. That
doesn't sound too democratic, or even encouraging. We need
to ask, "Who's to blame?" If you answered the non-committed, non-affiliated, non-voting public, you are right on target. Yes, these folks are the culprits. The party machine fears
your vote because, if organized, you could easily dictate the
outcome of an election. Maybe that would be sufficient to
send a strong message the political parties to run some decent candidates who know a little something. However, time
and time again the non-committed, non-affiliated and non-
voting public fails to cast ballots in any significant number
that could substantially affect the outcome of an election.
And the people who voted became discouraged, believing that
they have wasted their time in going to the polls, that their
vote didn't count for anything. If you believe this, then you
have played right into the hands of those proponents and
bosses of the two-party system. You have become an unwill-
ing enabler in the perpetuating of this political machine that
breeds mediocrity. You are doing exactly what the political

machine wants you to do and they didn't even lift a finger to help you. You did it all by yourself!

It is so tragic that we have become a nation of non-believers in the election process. It is easy to understand why the people become discouraged, yet simply acquiesce to the system that serves no productive purpose other than to perpetuate the election of mediocre, inept and unqualified individuals to represent you and to make decisions on your behalf. And in Gloucester County, we surely have had more then our share of unqualified candidates being elected over the years, the most glaring example recorded in recent years as noted in local, county and the state elections of 2000, 2002 and 2003. What was the public thinking?

Only you can change the system—perhaps not in one, two or even three elections, but if you stay the course, the change for the better will happen and that's a guarantee. The initial steps require everyone 18 years of age to register to vote; the second step is to initially register independent so that your vote can count in the general election and really make a difference; third, vote in every general election, school board election and special election. And if you don't vote, the power brokers simply interpret that failure on your behalf as a validation of the status quo. The Democrat and Republican machines will remain alive and healthy until the day that non-partisan elections become the norm, not the anomaly in this country. Although non-partisan political elections do exist in several municipalities, they do not exist at the County level or in the majority of municipal elections. Frankly, this type of open election will always meet with opposition from the political bosses and has little chance of ever being adopted by the State as the model for all municipal and county elections. Imagine if New Jersey were so bold to take that step in changing the manner in which the public elected officials? Imagine if New Jersey even took it one step further and applied non-partisan elections to the State Assembly and Senate races? We would definitely see some new faces on the political scene, and we would find many more voters coming to the polls.

Until there is change that benefits even the disenfranchised voters who refuse to align themselves with any specific political party, the best we can ask is that all members of the public keep themselves informed as to what is happening in the governments that serve them. This will take some effort on the part of the public. You must know the names of your elected officials and perhaps even recognize them by sight. Attending a meeting, especially at budget time, is essential so that you realize what is happening with your hard-earned dollars that you pay in taxes. And I caution the public that if you decline to become personally involved as mentioned above, at least question the sources from which you glean information. Many sources of so-called "information" are at best dubious, if not prejudicial. Among those dubious sources I include the press, a neighbor, political mailings and the infamous *letters to the editor,* the latter being the most unreliable, eclipsed only by comments from a newspapers editorial staff.

As a person who has committed his entire life to public and community service, I cannot understand why residents don't care enough to get involved in their community to at least the bare minimum. How one can vote for a candidate not knowing the real person and basing an opinion on the comments of adversaries and/or supporters or the press escapes me. What you hear is not always the truth and more often than not, it's a fabrication. I would always welcome the opportunity to speak with and meet the public face to face. I was perhaps one of a handful of South Jersey politicians who were highly visible and had well over an 90% name recognition rating just after three years into my first term as mayor. I made a point of walking neighborhoods and knocking on doors during non-election years. I was often amused with the comments shared by many residents, "The only time I see you is at election time" (usually followed by a snarl or laughter). My response, unlike many vote-beggars, was not apologetic: "I was doing my job, working for the community and if you needed me, I was but a phone call or a postage stamp away." As far as I was concerned, the discussion was over! There was nothing more to say.

Many times residents who wanted to engage in a debate on issues at the front door probably didn't care enough to gather their thoughts and present those questions at a more appropriate time and in the proper venue. These residents are either not registered to vote, vote only the party line, or don't vote. They wouldn't give you a vote no matter how much sense you made in explaining any issue. And in some cases, I found some people to be simply angry, unhappy or just plain cantankerous. Time to move on to another door because that door is closed, either on a political, emotional or intellectual basis.

There are times, however, when a community can generate sufficient anger to mobilize for change. It isn't often that this will happen, but Washington Township has had two such events occur. The first instance was related to a time when there was a challenge to moral virtues. Our churches and synagogues may not be bursting at the seams, much to the dismay of pastors and rabbis, but the thought of our community being attacked by the purveyors of sex and immorality was A CALL TO ARMS. The second event brought the long-standing government to its knees and booted it out of Town Hall, along with several politicians who had worn out their welcome and frankly, their usefulness as public leaders. The stories of those events follow.

Chapter 6

STAND UP AND FIGHT

Two issues polarized this community to the point of excess. In one of those situations cooler heads *did not* prevail and several individuals, believed to be well-intentioned, simply turned a deaf ear and a blind eye to what was happening nationwide. The United States of America was changing and morality was being set aside by the courts in deference to free expression with an absence of parameters. The sexual revolution was gaining momentum and the "Chablis and me generation" had begun to take hold. Changes were on the horizon.

The Route 42 Plaza Cinema and the Gemini Bookstore attacked the very fiber of the community. It seemed as though pornography was something that the residents of Washington Township would not stand for under any circumstances. You would expect that the clergy would definitely stand against such an attack on all that is decent and moral. As the issue intensified, we came to see a cadre of other individuals posing as bastions of the moral order, hoping to gain the proper level of exposure in order to lay the foundation for a future political campaign. Not very altruistic, but you couldn't possibly expect more from a politician, could you?

As anticipated, the troops mobilized with placards and signs in what would be considered a peaceful demonstration against the management of the Plaza 42 Cinema. Many times, in silence, there is strength. It was quite obvious that the men frequenting this XXX-rated theater wanted to ensure that they were not recognized or photographed for fear of being labeled by the public as a pervert. As an interested citizen, a teacher of Catholic Doctrine and as a member of the School Board, I too was very concerned that the ONE theater in our community was XXX-rated. What does that say about us as a people? A community? I made sure that I instructed my CCD students in the appropriate method of demonstration and of course, the issue and its impact on a community if not properly controlled. I stood with my students in demonstrating. As high school-aged kids they needed to understand the ramifications of the Supreme Court's ruling on this issue and how the decision would become inextricably immersed in the First Amendment and therefore, this was only the tip of the proverbial iceberg and was a foreshadowing of what would occur in years to come nationwide. This was a perfect opportunity to teach young people the need to stand up and be counted when other means of resolving an emerging problem fail. Such demonstrations need to be carried out properly, so the demonstration won't be depicted as irrational, ignorant or simply a gaggle of fools looking for their 15 minutes of fame.

I must admit that I was concerned with the Township Committee's lack of success in attracting more industrial and commercial ratables and of course, that included more than ONE cinema and three legitimate restaurants to the town. Except for strip malls, the Township Committee had done very little to provide respectable shopping areas and specialty stores in order to support the ever-growing number of residents moving into the Township weekly. No Master Plan or commercial/industrial development plan seemed apparent, nor was one visible to the average citizen. The tax burden of paying for services and the growing school district was falling squarely on the shoulders of the homeowners. The local school district's future seemed to be in jeopardy as school budgets met with defeat as voters tried to control the runaway taxes caused by the lack of commercial and industrial ratables. The only people benefiting by this lack of leadership from Town Hall were residential developers who walked in the front door with plans and out the back door with approvals.

To make my case for what I believe to be one of the darker times in this Township's political and abusive control of Township Committee, let's reflect on the farmland tract that is now the location of Plaza 42. The farmland was owned by a holding company of which the Township's solicitor was a principal partner. The approval as to the number and size of the signs on that site was without precedent. One of the larger signs and in fact the first sign seen by visitors at the time was the Plaza 42 Cinema sign. As previously stated, this sign's size was unprecedented and never to be replicated, at least through my administration. The ineptness of the Planning Board in not questioning the freestanding Cinema 42 sign as well as a freestanding building set to the back-lot property line of the site to be hidden by all other construction is suspect. The fact that a road hugging the northwest property line that traversed behind the rear of several other buildings was permitted is also suspect. As if that weren't enough of a clue that something wasn't quite right, the plans for the interior and exterior of the cinema described a small and limited lobby, a flat single-screened theatre, and a rather drab entrance that even to the most unaesthetic eye did not cry out a "family theater." Sorry to say it folks, but the Township Committee and Planning Board of the 1970's were asleep when this project got approved. But then again politics played a major role in rubber stamping this blight on our community.

After the demonstrations and other negative publicity that surrounded the operations of theater, the owner agreed to show family movies as long as the community gave its support. "Well, why not?" said the protectors of our morality and thus a deal was struck to close the XXX-rated theater and to make it a family theater. Of course, every one of the politicians, as well as the wannabe politicians and organizers of the protests, fell over themselves trying to get the credit for this major coup and to capture a headline or two. Well, as they say, nothing is quite as it appears to be! In order to show first-run or at least quality films, you need to convince a distributor that the house has the technical and cinematic requirements to show the size and quality of films that were being produced at that time. The Cinema 42 failed all these requirements. After about three months showing of second-rate, low-budget films, the crowds evaporated, the protest-ors retreated into silence and the Plaza 42 Cinema showed XXX-rated, adult films.

(I was personally pleased to bring to an end the era of the Plaza 42 Cinema. It took time, but I never took my eye off the target. I made a commitment in the 1970's that took al-most 20 years to fulfill. But I did it and I did it alone, without any fanfare or support. I'll discuss this aspect of my political career in the section "The Arduous Times."

Chapter 7

STAND UP AND FIGHT...
WITH WEAPONS?

T
he next battle undertaken by the community was somewhat less restrained and far from what we would consider civil conduct. Another dark time in this community's history prompted extremely uncivilized actions, rivaled only by several Township Committee meetings in the 1980's or several meetings in 1999 and 2000 conducted by Councilmen Rapposelli or Lyons (who should know better since they are attorneys). In all these instances, insanity was orchestrated for several reasons. And if you guessed that these actions were premeditated and carefully orchestrated for the sole purpose of politics before the people, you are absolutely and unequivocally correct! So what else is new in this community!

The calamity discussed here was of sufficient magnitude to force a referendum initiated by the people that would change the form of government, booting out some very unpopular politicians and their appointed solicitor. We also saw Township meetings that resulted in actual physical contact between residents, between elected officials and between residents and elected officials. The Township's meetings were referred to as The Circus. This community was made the laughingstock of all South Jersey. Thanks to the vested interest and personal agendas of the elected officials, their cronies, the party leadership—both Democrat and Republican—and a group of contemptible and malevolent individuals who were members of the Board of Education, the Township was on a slippery slope. The roller coaster ride was all down hill and it was not good for the community or its residents. Something of this magnitude was repeated in 1999 and 2000 by the Democrat-controlled Council with Councilpersons Davidson, Lyons and Rapposelli, coached by the late Township attorney Jack Trimble and Assemblyman Bob Smith in doing what it took, regardless of the negativity and lies, to oust me from office. Regrettably, the plan worked because too many people didn't seek out the truth for themselves, but rather relied on the inaccuracy and prejudice of the reports in the press and the negative, well-funded campaigns of Assemblyman Bob Smith and mayoral candidate Councilperson Randee Davidson.

Under the umbrella of the First Amendment you will find not only do we argue the right of the free press and freedom of speech, but also the right for sexually explicit gift stores, book stores, adult movies, video rental stores, unisex boutiques, topless bars, gentlemen's clubs, strip clubs and more— all under the very broad term of *pornography*. This issue of pornography is so important to some that it was included in the campaign literature of Randee Davidson in 2000 (of course no one ever got the point of it since it was pointless).

In the early 1980's, the general public was not too keen on the liberalism that was beginning to polarize this nation. The courts became a little too liberal for those who had strong religious beliefs, regardless of their religious affiliation. Times were changing and a lot of folks were not ready for this kind of change. Like many, I believed the Supreme Court to be too liberal, but then again, the failure of the highest Court in the land to respond to the will of the people is due primarily to the fact that a lifetime appointment to a position of such authority and power can breed complacency as well as the most serious of illnesses affecting political appointees, the "out of touch with reality" malady of which the only known cure is to throw the bums out!

The owners of the Gemini Book Store had selected a site fronting on Route 42 at the farthest southeasterly boundary of the Township, so far removed from the hub of the community that some thought the location to be in neighboring Monroe Township. The area was dominated even at that time with the beginnings of car dealerships, there was a great deal of vacant land that was choice for commercial and industrial development. The only residential growth immediately adjacent to the site was a small area of single-family homes, a mobile home park, a stand-alone motel and store or two. This section was called Cross/Keys Mayfair and the street names were reminiscent of a section of Philadelphia. The homes were modest and far from the pretentious homes that were under construction in many sections of the community. This type of social separation was the catalyst for the reaction that was to arise from the location of the Gemini Bookstore.

Whenever a neighborhood in any community, no matter in what town, or state in suburbia, USA, feels as though they are being put upon for whatever reason, you can predict the response to be one of the following: "Sure, why not us—we're the forgotten neighborhood" "None of the neighborhoods with expensive homes get disrespected" "We always get the left-overs" and the one response that has become identified with suburbia, USA,—"Not in my backyard." (ergo the term NIMBY). These attitudes will never change because this is part of human nature and once inculcated in the collective mind of the residents, no amount of logic will ever change that, and I speak from experience. I have been there and done that! Logic has no place here. The residents simply want it their way and short of that, any solution is considered a sell-out.

The public crowded into the old municipal building for several heated debates on the Gemini Book Store. This time in the 1980's was not necessarily a productive time for the Township. Politics, residential growth, developers failing to meet commitments to the people who purchased their homes, a school board in turmoil and a Municipal Utilities Authority led by a czar who showed nothing but contempt towards the people, simply had the residents in a state of agitation, anger, despair and frustration. The pot had reached a boil!

The first shots were fired at Township Committee meetings. Angry residents shook their fists, shouted obscenities and hurled accusations of the most insulting kind at committee persons. More than once the Chairman's gavel would strike the table so often as to sound like a sledge hammer on a slab of concrete, attempting to control an unruly standing-room-only crowd almost on the brink of becoming an angry mob, flirting with the idea of taking matters into their own hands. Too often was it necessary to have the police eject residents into the parking lot, where fights erupted between angry men and screaming women under the eager eyes of newspaper reporters whose cameras encouraged these people to seek their moment of fame or at least to see their picture in tomorrow's newspaper.

Inside the building, the committeepersons fought among themselves, shaking fists, name calling, using profanity and resorting to physical violence, which simply polarized the crowd into a frenzy. Attempts by the Township solicitor to recite the First Amendment or to explain to the crowd the Supreme Court's position on adult bookstores was met with hisses, boos and other anti-government slogans and attorney-bashing comments. The lack of leadership among the elected officials and their inability to stand up by telling it like it is regardless of the political fallout was obvious. The voices of reason were never heard above the roar of the crowd, which now resembled a mob of thugs.

In defense of the many respectable residents of this community, they sought answers and got questions; they sought reason and found the unreasonable; they looked for guidance and found rhetoric; they asked salient questions and were patronized; they sought a leader and found only pos-

Gerald J. Luongo, Ph.D.

turing politicians blaming others and accepting none of the responsibility to effect a solution. Perhaps no solution would address the anger, the concern, the feelings of frustration and violation. What next?

Committeeman and then appointed Mayor Anthony Sebastiano (deceased) attempted to address this nagging, divisive issue in earnest. He looked to other communities in and outside of New Jersey for answers and for a solution. His research led him to a possible compromise—not the perfect solution but at least it was a plan that would control the spread of this malignancy that was here to stay regardless of what the people wanted. Sebastiano's plan did require a sacrifice from some residents but the over-whelming majority of citizens would benefit and so would the community as a whole. Of course all opposing forces would need to face the reality that adult bookstores were legal under the law of the land. The decision to permit or deny such a business was not in the purview of elected officials. The best that they could hope for was the control to establish parameters that would insulate the community to the greatest degree possible from its presence.

Mayor Sebastiano met with the solicitor. His plan had its basis in case law that was challenged in other communities. Armed with what he believed to be the solution, he announced his plan at a public meeting. Washington Township would create a zone specifically permitting adult entertainment and excluding such adult-centered entertainment from commercial zones. It was the only solution afforded that would pass legal muster, avoiding the many lawsuits that would most assuredly ensue. Sebastiano did not want to make Washington Township the precedent for the law books or create a financial feeding frenzy for the lawyers. Although his confidant and attorney Jack Trimble (deceased) was an aggressive lawyer, he had a mediocre record in the win column and was too combative, something that would define him for the next two decades. Sebastiano nevertheless decided to move forward, deciding it was time to begin the healing process for the community regardless of the political suicide that he was about to commit.

Unfortunately this last, earnest effort to address the problem failed. Sebastiano received little support and much ridicule of his plan. His detractors, including members of the Township's Police Department, carefully orchestrated what would be his eventual demise in politics.

The impatience of the crowd attending all these meetings finally erupted into a scene that would rival even a Hollywood movie or at least the Jerry Springer Show. Fueled by certain unethical members of the press and by several unscrupulous politicians (and we had plenty of them), the crowd, led by a few self-appointed, self-righteous protectors of morality, determined that a frontal attack on the evil bookstore was the answer. Likened to a mob of villagers armed with clubs and torches following the town's burgomeister in pursuit of Frankenstein, a mob of township people carried baseball bats, flashlights and signs. The arrival of key politicians for photo-ops and their words of encouragement were greeted with enthusiasm. Of course, once the press and the photographers left to make their deadline, the politicians did too.

The demonstration ended, the people returned home and to this day, the Gemini Adult Book Store continues to serve its clientele. The result of all this melodrama and emotional upheaval did nothing positive for the residents or the community. Thanks to the press, the Township became the laughingstock of South Jersey, an image that took years to undo. Just what were these people thinking? And from all this confusion and ugliness came two things: the needed catalyst was provided in order to change the form of Township government, and two, the detractors of Tony Sebastiano got him ousted out of office. He unfortunately had stepped on too many toes, making employees accountable to the people, especially specific members of the Township's Police Department, and he simply refused to acquiesce to the demands of his own political party. Change was afoot!

Chapter 8

A Government is Born

After the melodrama of the Gemini Adult Book Store played itself out, the community seemingly entered a period of repose. During this period of time, a group of spirited and concerned individuals came together to form an exploratory committee to investigate the process for effecting a change of government for the community. These individuals were convinced that if the community had a mayor directly elected by the people, the response to the grievances of the people would be addressed in a more direct fashion, void of political interferences to the degree possible. The Committee form of government provided too much latitude in permitting elected officials the opportunity to pass the buck. With the Mayor/Council form of government, at least the buck would stop at the Mayor's desk. The exploratory committee had arrived at an astute and common-sense idea. For this form of government to succeed in Washington Township, the

Mayor would need to be the chief administrator of the government and the head of the executive branch while the Council of five members elected at large would be the legislative branch. A clear delineation of authority would exist and the Mayor would need to be a strong leader, which would be essential to the new government's success.

The employees, in general, supported this form of government. The Committee form of government appointed members of the Township Committee to act as directors of various departments in the government. In most cases, the politicians lacked the training or expertise to fill such a role. Many county forms of government continue to operate under this system and frankly, the level of employee productivity is, at best, average if not mediocre. This was the case in the community. The residents were entitled to a lot more, given the salaries being paid to the employees and the outstanding working conditions and benefits package provided. Those who work in government must understand that their first responsibility is to the people and that accountability to the people and one's superiors is paramount to the smooth and efficient operation of good government.

Especially supportive of this change in government was the police department. The department was fortunate to have a man of honor and integrity at its helm. Chief Fred Reeves encouraged a good interface between the men and women in blue and the community. Chief Reeves had a way with people that simply ingratiated him with the public. (Fred Reeves retired as Chief and moved on to head the Gloucester County Police Academy at the Gloucester County Community College. His retirement from that post in the late '90s created a void in leadership and personal integrity that would never be filled. His successor to the director's position was a retired Township police officer and political player who was rewarded for his role in several political and reprehensible subversive actions orchestrated by Freeholder Director Steve "Boss" Sweeney. The appointment was of course politically expedient, but it did little to provide the Academy with the kind of leadership established by Fred Reeves. Lloyd Dumont was, in my opinion and in the opinion of many Law Enforcement Personnel, the least-suited candidate for the job as Director of the Academy and was not even supported by the Gloucester County Police Chiefs. Dumont had been forced to resign from the prosecutor's office due to an incident involving an assault on another investigator and was hired on the rebound by the Township. Dumont was politically wise, having made all the right connections, eventually selling out to County Democrat leadership in order to have a title so sorely needed for his inflated ego.)

Under the Committee form of government, Chief Reeves had to deal with Tony Sebastiano on a daily basis. As a retired Philadelphia policeman, Sebastiano was of the mind that police personnel should be more aggressive, which was in direct opposition to the position that Reeves held. Given the laid-back and generally quiet nature of the community, the kinds of crimes found in the city on a regular basis were few and far between in the Township. With this in mind, Chief Reeves approached local policing more from the community policing standpoint, which in fact worked quite well in suburbia. Sebastiano especially found fault with the detective division, a concern that would carry on through the next two administrations. The conflict of the perceived interference with the police department by the township's elected leaders escalated, leading members of the police department into the political arena, many aligning themselves with Sebastiano's opposition with the promise of promotions and autonomy from governmental oversight. This was the beginning of Police in Politics and did not make for a healthy atmosphere nor was it appropriate in my opinion. (In future years, specifically the period dominated by the leadership of Councilpersons Matthew Lyons, Ray Rapposelli and Randee Davidson, the Police Department was used as puppets and pawns to the benefit of these politicians and their cronies. This type of abuse by these politicians virtually killed the morale of the officers and created isolated factions among the men and women in blue exemplified by distrust and disloyalty among the rank and file. The systematic destruction of the *spirit de corps* was further exacerbated by the appointment of Fran Burke in 2001 as Police Chief, a man that I purposely passed over as Chief two times. His dictatorial methods were unhealthy and of no value in improving the police department's role in this community. Burke, under orders from Council, used intimidation and fear coupled with divisiveness to ensure that every officer followed his dictums. His reign of terror is perhaps the darkest moment in this Township's history. His retirement in May of 2004 was a welcomed breath of fresh air to the department and to the community.)

The momentum for change in the mid 1980's moved quickly. The selling of this change of government came fairly easily. The majority of the residents comprising Washington Township came from the city and all they ever knew was the Mayor/Council form of government. Considering the abysmal record of accomplishments by the Committee that had been elected to date and the failure of any elected leader to provide a vision for the future, the binding referendum passed. In 1984, Washington Township embarked upon establishing a new form of government: a Mayor and five Councilpersons elected at large. The elections would be political with a primary election held in June and a general election in November. All terms would be four years with the Mayor and two Council seats coinciding with the Presidential election and three Council seats being voted upon two years later. This was the dawning of a new era in Washington Township government. Were the politicians ready?

Chapter 9

GROWING PAINS–
THE FIRST ELECTION

The political parties hit the ground running in the early part of 1985 as they prepared to capture the Mayor's seat and five Council seats in the November election. The June primary had no shortage of candidates on either side of the aisle. Under the old form of government, primaries were boring—the slate was seldom challenged and frankly, except for the rank and file faithful, primary turn-outs were poor. But the primary of 1985 proved to be an anomaly, and the result was change in the balance of power, with the party taking a secondary role to the candidates. It seemed as though the electorate began to examine candidates more closely, not necessarily voting the party line. The use of paper ballots made it easier not to vote the party line as compared to the punch-card system for balloting that followed. Due to the voter-rich base in Washington Township, the County always counted these ballots last, as this vote could dictate the outcome of an election. I am sure that part of the reason for this was that the Township was always slow in delivering the completed ballots to the County Election headquarters. As the County prepared to move into the 21st century, electronic touch-screen voting machines were introduced in the 1990's and election results could be finalized by 10 p.m.

My memory may be somewhat fuzzy on the precise details of that famous primary, but there were at least 18 candidates running for Council and four candidates for Mayor. Local committeepersons were on the ballot, with several new names and faces added into the mix. The issues included residential growth, taxes, the adult book store and adult theater, lack of commercial growth and industrial development, quality and quantity of the Township's water supply, failure to provide sanitary sewers throughout the Township, and numerous complaints relative to incomplete housing developments, drainage, road conditions and planning. Many issues that had never been addressed in the past years were now resurfacing and begging to be dealt with. Whoever would be elected had their work cut out for them. We could only hope that our government was prepared to take on the challenge. Only time would tell. A spirited general election loomed in the offing.

The summer of 1985 was relatively quiet as to politics. The Fourth of July parade did bring to the public's eye a plethora of political floats, politicians and candidates. This parade was one of the Township's proudest moments, organized and run by volunteers who worked hard and put in many hours in making this parade South Jersey's premier parade. Everyone wanted to part of a winning situation. Campaign slogans abounded and many of the political floats displayed many hours of preparation. Of course, in Washington Township where extremes are seemingly the norm, other candidates were obvious by their lack of any innovative or creative ideas in their presentation. As the announcer for that parade and a proud member of the committee, I watched the parade from the reviewing stand located in front of Sal's Pizza at the intersection of Greentree and Egg Harbor Roads. I announced with enthusiasm each and every organization, including the candidates running for office. You could see just how hard they were working to make sure that the voters remembered them on election day in November. Getting out the vote and selling your message would be the key to the election of '85.

As summer turned to fall and the late afternoons brought about a fresh briskness in the air, campaigns took to the streets, with candidates knocking on doors and sharing their vision for a better community. In truth, many of the candidates didn't have a clue as to what was going on or, worse yet, any plans to solve many of the issues facing the Township. These candidates simply wanted to get elected. In several cases they wanted what they perceived as the *power* to even political scores. Perhaps these candidates were sincere individuals but their reasons and motives for seeking public office were all wrong. Many of the candidates focused on criticizing the Municipal Utilities Authority, the Township's independent money-making authority. Water and sanitary sewer rates were some of the highest in the area and their attentiveness and response to the public on issues was the lowest in the area. The MUA needed seminars in interfacing with the public and how to respond to their subscribers in a polite and professional manner. The appointed and politically charged board of directors lacked, for the most part, any skills dealing with the public.

The inability for the MUA to successfully communicate with the public was due in large part to the dictatorial leadership of Val Orsimarsi, a Republican Party leader who was able to maneuver the political minefields, surviving both Democratic and Republican administrations. His political savvy and his loyalty to no one but himself enabled him to work deals with both parties that always benefited him first. He was dubbed, "the water czar." His legacy would continue well on into my administration, as did the problems that the MUA had with its image. Although the Democrats running for election in 1998 vowed to change the operations of the MUA when they gained control, they too failed to do anything except not to reappoint Orsimarsi. Lyons, Rapposelli and Davidson saw the benefit of keeping the MUA just the way it was and used it to their political and financial advantage. Appointments to the MUA board were choice political plums and reserved for those loyal and obedient Democrats and Republicans who served their party well. These rewards were costly in many ways. The professionals appointed by the MUA board included engineers, lawyers and accountants and they too paid a price for their appointment. These professionals, as a matter of fact, were appointed predicated on the amount and frequency of contributions made to the party coffers. People so often forget that politics is a business and the business cannot operate without dollars to run campaigns. Money is the fuel that drives the political engine and if you think otherwise, you are so very wrong.

Chapter 10

POLITICAL DIRTY TRICKS

N o book dealing with any aspect of politics remembered would be complete without talking about some of the dirty tricks that politicians and their cronies would do to get elected. Depending on how much I can stomach as I dig deep into the annals of my mind, I will share. Now you might think that statement to be rather self-serving, or at least cavalier. It implies that I have never been a part of dirty politics. And it also implies that there is a clean side to politics. And to both of these statements I answer, "Yes."

Regrettably the intensity of ugly or dirty politics has escalated to a point in our society that most people now anticipate it, expect it and, unfortunately, accept it. Politics today has become an ugly battleground where name calling, lies, innuendo, gossip, inaccurate reporting and distortions of the truth and facts have become commonplace. Issues are in the background while the circus atmosphere of the campaign takes front stage. Could this be due to the fact that many of the politicians have nothing salient to say? Perhaps they are ignorant of the issues and worse yet, they might not even know how to address the issues in an intelligent and articulate fashion. Most politicians running for office do not have solutions to problems, just criticisms of the other candidate. They insult the intelligence of the astute voter who is attempting to extrapolate the facts from the piles of garbage that the press and the political gurus try to feed them every day. And so many politicians do this without a conscience as to the damage they do. They dismiss any criticism of their inappropriate, stupid and buffoonish actions by saying, "It's only politics."

I can say without equivocation I have never engaged in dirty politics. I made a decision early on in my political career that I would take the high road and stay focused on the issues. In my literature I would face the issues head on and offer, in writing, the solutions. I was not afraid to tell the people what I would do once elected. Why surprise them? I wanted their vote ONLY if they really believed in me. That is what I call clean politics. I am not interested, nor have I ever been interested, in attacking personally any individual who opposed me in an election. I respect the fact that they too have families and after the election is history, these individuals have to go back to their families, neighbors, friends and colleagues. No need to hurt people unnecessarily. Although I have been the victim of some very ugly, even vile personal attacks in every election in which I have participated, I have never responded in kind. My personal compass is firmly entrenched in Christian values. One does not go out of one's way to hurt others for the sake of advancing one's self at any cost, especially when there is an absence of fact and documentation to prove the allegations. Inaccuracy in political campaigns is as common as the cold and as annoying and insidious. I have seen respectable people succumb to dirty politics for many reasons, most of them related to money, position or power. I have seen far too many people cast aside their integrity just to be part of what they believed to be the winning team and to curry favor with the victor. I have seen people who I trusted do the most contemptible acts in the name of politics. Selling themselves out for whatever and become nothing but a puppet or a pawn of some very unscrupulous people. How very pathetic and sad that anyone would sell out so cheaply with little or no regard for their personal integrity. And as much as these people think that this is a well-kept secret, they are so very wrong. Anyone with good sense knows what and who you are. These miscreants come from all walks of life and all occupations and professions. What will always separate people like that from the honest hardworking politicians is the respect of the people who know the truth. Yes, the truth that will always rise to the surface, no matter what kind of spin the liars try to put on it. People who know the truth will always look at the liars for what they represent—the worst in the human element. Amazing how these people dismiss the voice of their conscience and set aside any religious values which they may have had at one time. But then again, I think that I have answered my concerns: perhaps this ugly side of the human element is without conscience and holds to no religious value. That would make perfect sense! With this kind of person, karma will deal with them at the appropriate time. Life has a way of balancing the scales of justice and we humans have no need to get involved.

One cannot omit from the list of dirty political tricks the one that took place during the election of 1985. This hurt an entire family. Whether or not the persons responsible for doing this took the time to think through the consequences of their actions will remain a mystery. The time was the general election of 1985 when John Robertson was the Democratic candidate for Mayor and Sally Cummins the Republican candidate in the first election under the new form of government. This would be Washington Township's first Mayor elected directly by the people.

The Democrats in Washington Township were never at a loss at finding ways of attacking people, no matter what the cost and this was prior to the time that it was fashionable. For years, their loud, offensive and bullish conduct did very little to enhance the image of the community. Fistfights, name calling, obscenities and your garden variety of dirty tricks defined the Democrat Party generally speaking throughout Gloucester County. From what I have seen even to this day, not much has changed. And I hasten to add I was a registered Democrat from the day that my family and I moved to the Township in 1969 until I moved to the Republican Party in 1995. Frankly I'd had enough and the leadership of the

Democrat Party and its philosophy wasn't about to change, so it was time for me and my supporters to move on.

The Screamer was a favorite tool of the Democrat Party and also some unsavory on the fringe Republican Politicians who some of you may remember: Mary Virginia "Ginny" Weber and her sidekick Bob Berry (deceased) and their merry band of troublemakers. *The Screamer* was a tabloid newspaper that would rival *The Enquirer* and the *The Star*. Distorted photos, twisted stories, fiction not facts, quotes attributed to nonexistent people, lies, innuendos, half-truths and pasted-up actual headlines from area newspapers but with fictitious stories. All this was printed with every assurance that it was the Gospel truth! The printing of this rag usually began in the late evening on a Sunday and carried over into early Monday morning, the day before the election. Then in the cover of darkness between 2 a.m. and 5 a.m. on the day of the election, a group of diehard party supporters would descend upon the community like a swarm of locusts, stuffing mailboxes and front doors with this trash. *The Screamer* did irrevocable harm to many good people, not just at the polls but to their reputation.

Like many others who have made a study of New Jersey's voting publics' profiles, I have come to the conclusion that many people are turned off by negative campaigning and do not vote. For those who do vote, regardless of the political climate, some 40% are directly affected by negative campaign literature and subscribe to the theory that all of it can't be lies. *The Screamer* did much to discourage good people from seeking office. For those of us it did not discourage, we simply suffered in silence through all the attacks before and after election time.

Sally Cummins and her family moved to Washington Township from out of state. She became involved with the Republican Party, as did her husband. In the 1980's the Republican Party was not necessarily strong and unfortunately was dominated by a few people whose motto, "My way or no way," did little to increase Republican Party membership or registrations. The depth of possible candidates to oppose the well-liked, intelligent and articulate Democrat John Robertson were few to none. This lack of a potential candidate was due to the past record of the Republican Party, which had difficulty in getting candidates elected in previous elections. So often Republican candidates were on track to reach the finish line as winners. However, during the final weeks of the campaign, something uncanny would happen. The financial resources would diminish and the support of the rank and file would seemingly begin to evaporate. The leadership of the Republican Party did little to revive the campaign. It is common belief among many people who have lived through this actual scenario, that the Republican leadership was always making deals that required them to sell out one of their own. Considering how some Republicans have done personally, the belief has become quite plausible.

As the campaign of 1985 unfolded, Sally Cummins held to the theme that Robertson was part of the problems in the community and not the solution. His service on Township Committee, in her opinion, demonstrated his inability to work well with others and to solve the problems facing the community. Robertson in his own defense pointed with pride to his ability to indeed work with the public, to interact with some very disagreeable politicians and to work with County and State officials. Robertson was a college graduate and as far as politics was concerned, he was a seasoned trooper. Ms. Cummins was a political neophyte. She was part of the Change of Government Petition process, but she still lacked the political acumen needed for the rough-and-tumble politics of this community. Frankly, her chances of beating Robertson at the polls were very slight and should have not been of any concern to the Democratic Party. The Republicans lacked the finances and the organization to get out the vote. Nevertheless the ugliness of a few mean-spirited Democrats could not be contained and surfaced as a clandestine operation not under the Party's banner. This attack on Ms. Cummins would lead her and the family to move out of the community.

It seems that there has always been a double standard in politics. No one ever questions why a man jumps into the political arena and it is expected that his spouse will be there for him. When a woman decides to get involved, there are always questions as to why she is doing this. Perhaps she is unhappy with her husband or tired of her responsibilities as a mother and wife, or perhaps she enjoys being out of the house sharing time with the many men in the political arena. Well, given that ignorant and chauvinist thinking, a group of unscrupulous, irresponsible reprobates hatched a plan. Realizing that Mr. Cummins would be home alone with the children more times than not, preparing dinner, putting the kids to bed and whatever, these creeps called the house when his wife was out on the campaign trail. At first the calls resulted in hang-ups, which can be most annoying. When you as a husband or a wife begin to realize that these calls only occur when one of the partners is out of the home, your mind can conjure up some doubts as to what is going on! However, love and trust usually overcomes all doubts.

Later, the male caller would ask for "Sally." When her husband asked who was calling or whether he would like to leave a message, the caller would say no and abruptly hang up. Eventually the calls escalated to callers asking the husband if he knew where his wife was and what she was doing. At the same time rumors were leaked to the public and to the press indicating problems at the Cummins' home, possibly infidelity and a pending divorce. Before long the lies became the accepted truth and Sally Cummins was spoken of in less than flattering terms throughout the community. How tragic, how reprehensible, how ugly.

After her loss to Robertson in November of 1985, the Cummins family moved from the community in the late spring of 1986. A few years later my suspicions as to who were the culprits in this dastardly deed were confirmed when one of the miscreants boasted about what he done. That person and I became enemies until his death a few years ago. I choose not to mention his name as not to further embarrass the family, whose respect of their father was obligatory at best. We do not sit in judgment of our fellow man. There is a higher authority to whom we will all answer someday and at that time, the ledger of life will be balanced.

Chapter 11

THE FORMATIVE FOUR

I n January of 1986 John Robertson was sworn in as the Township's first elected Mayor. The five Council members were also sworn in and seated. These elected officials would establish the administrative guidelines that would govern this community. The Council elected a President and Vice-President along party lines. It was also necessary for the Clerk to conduct a drawing to determine who would have the full four years in office and who would need to run again in two years in order to gain a full term of four years. There would be two full-term seats running concurrent with the Mayor's term of four years, and three seats that would be elected during the second year of the Mayor's term and the two council members' terms. Once this was done, the election cycle would take care of the process.

New Jersey statutes provide nine forms of government under the Faulkner Act. Within the statutes, specific duties and responsibilities are enumerated for the executive and legislative branches of government. The Township voters selected a strong Mayor (executive branch) and a weak Council (legislative branch) form of government. The document that would clearly delineate the powers of each branch of government would be the Administrative Code. This document would be questioned and challenged every year well into my administration. Like John Robertson, I held to the Administrative Code and never equivocated to Council, which always wanted more power. (In 2001 Council began to systematically strip Mayor Randee Davidson of many powers that were her responsibility as defined in the Administrative Code. However, it was apparent that Davidson did not have an understanding, the intellectual ability or the desire to be an effective mayor and executive leader of this community and therefore, willingly acquiesced and abdicated, thus relegating herself to being a ceremonial mayor. This resulted in her not having to make any of the tough decisions. This puppet form of government worked quite well for the Democrat-controlled Council, which was manipulated by the county Democratic bosses and local Councilman Matthew Lyons, former Councilman Raymond Rapposelli and township solicitor John Trimble, Jr. (recently deceased.)

This form of government designates the Council as the voting body, which could enact and/or repeal the laws (ordinances) that govern the community. Any action of this type requires a series of public readings, advertisements and public hearings. The Mayor held the right to veto any of the ordinances promulgated by Council. To override that veto, Council would need four votes. However, no changes to the Administrative Code could be made that were in direct conflict with the statutes of the State of New Jersey. The Mayor would have no vote on any issue except to break a tie in filling a vacancy on Council. The Mayor was also entitled to all rights and privileges granted a Council person in having full participation in all Council meetings. Also, the Mayor was entitled to the Courtesy of the Floor, by law, and not at the discretion of the Council President. (Both Lyons and Rapposelli, with the support of Davidson, tried in vain to deny me those rights in the last two years that I was Mayor. All this was to no avail since I never did acquiesce to threats and bullies and especially to ignorant and rude people.) The Mayor retained the authority to appoint the vast majority of professionals serving the Township as well as the majority of volunteer boards. The Council appointed the auditor, members of the Zoning Board and members to the Municipalities Utilities Authority. (The latter two boards always caused a problem, no matter which political party appointed them. I believe that this was due to the member's lack of skills in dealing with the public as well as an inflated sense of personal importance). The Administrative Code would be challenged for years, if not by Council members then by the uninformed public. It seemed that many Council members and members of the public either couldn't understand the basic outline of the document or simply chose to ignore the Administrative Code's content for purely political reasons. The law was simple, not complicated and after all, this is what the people voted for in 1985. Regrettably this kind of provincial mindset becomes a major obstacle to efficient government, creating many unnecessary and orchestrated conflicts that were singularly designed for the purpose of Council members' self-aggrandizement, political posturing or grabbing a headline or two and anyone's expense. Many Council members and their cronies contributed absolutely nothing to this community, and their services can be only categorized as mediocre and prosaic. We were, however, fortunate to have some very good people serving on Council and their contributions are still working today in keeping this township a Premier Community.

John Robertson was the perfect choice for this Township's first elected mayor. He brought to the position many positive, innate and intuitive personal characteristics that were needed to lead this community. Robertson held a degree in Criminal Justice and through his employment at the county level of government, he understood Gloucester County both as a professional and a native. His ability to write and speak in an articulate fashion and his personal presence brought to the office a professional demeanor that was lacking for many years in government. His keen sense of humor, interpersonal skills, leadership style and executive management ability defined his temerity that would enable him to do so much for the people and the community.

Mayor Robertson immediately took on the challenges of the mayor's office. He made the professional appointments of community-oriented people to positions that would best serve all the people of the Township in a responsible and respectable fashion. Throughout his four-year term, he made changes in personnel that pleased some and disappointed others. Although he could be fiercely political, he refused to be a puppet of the Democratic Party (a position that never sits well with Party leadership). He did not discuss appointments or personnel hiring with the party chairman, which seriously diminishes the party chairman's power.

Mayor Robertson and Washington Township were an ideal marriage as the community began to explore uncharted waters. Unfortunately, the Mayor would find that the waters were swarming with barracuda of the Republican and Democratic variety as well as a special species called the press (aka Maureen Graham). As politically astute as Robertson may have been, he could have never anticipated that a Brutus lurked in the shadows.

Chapter 12

DEVELOPERS AND ECONOMIC DEVELOPMENT— NAUGHTY WORDS?

I n Washington Township why do people associate the word developer with something that is negative? In Roget's *21st Century Thesaurus* you cannot find one negative synonym for it. Imagine, not ONE negative synonym, yet in this community, the word developer is consider something evil— something to fear and to shun at all costs. Perhaps the head lexicographer at the Princeton Institute of Language has made a mistake. What this is all about is that the folks in this community, as in other communities, attribute negative connotations to a positive word by association, not definition. If the association is repeated sufficient times, it is then misconstrued as a definition.

When the average person thinks about the words developer and development, he immediately associates those terms with more homes, more traffic, more people, more school kids, less open space and perhaps more government. However, just for the purpose of making a point, let's set aside any preconceived notions or emotionality and muse objectively and rationally for a moment, thinking about these questions:

- Why did you move to Washington Township or any suburban community?

- Did you purchase a home in one of the many developments in the community?

- Did you plan to relocate here to lessen your commute to work?

- Did you ever investigate any of the mass transit alternatives?

- How many vehicles does your family have, including those used by kids away at college who come home to visit for longer than a week?

- If you have children, did you ever consider how they would get to school?

- Other than the home you purchased and the property on which it is constructed, did you buy any adjacent property as to guarantee your view of a farm or undeveloped land?

- Did you ever confirm the authenticity and accuracy of the architect's rendering of your entire development? Not the picture on the brochure or in the advertisement, but the approved plans on file at the municipal building?

- Regardless of your research prior to moving here, did you really believe in your heart that yours should be the last development approved?

- Did you really believe that no one else had the same rights as you to find a better place to call home for their family?

- If you own land, do you think that you are entitled to sell it or to develop it in order to make a profit as long as what you are going to develop is consistent with the community's Master Plan or Zoning Plan?

- Other than hearing the politicians, the malcontents and the wannabe politicians drone on about the Master Plan, do you know what it is and have you ever gone to your municipal building to read it?

- Seeing the number of developments in various stages of construction or the number of for sale signs on vacant land, didn't you realize that more development was imminent?

- Did you honestly believe that the vacant land adjacent to you property was forever going to be vacant?

- Isn't it necessary to have commercial development in order to provide retail, professional, entertainment, and health support services for the residents?

- Do you believe that residential property taxes ALONE could support public services and the educational system?

Many of these questions, framed differently, are the very same questions that planners, developers and land speculators ask themselves BEFORE they invest in a community. Do you have any idea how long it may take a land developer to capitalize on his investment? Do you know how long and how expensive the approval process can be when there are legal entanglements or lawsuits or worse yet, interference by the politicians who will do anything to curry a few votes when they know what they are doing is a sham?

I fail to understand why residential homeowners have such a difficult time in understanding that developers can only buy land that is for sale. Most of the land for sale in emerging suburbia is land owned by the old farmer down the road who is eagerly waiting for a developer to take an option on his land. Once that happens, the farmer is receiving a monthly check while still owning the land and perhaps even farming it. In the meantime, the developer is playing the waiting game, gambling as to how long it will be before he can get the town's approvals while continuing to pay the farmer, engineers, planners and a host of other professionals who are grazing at the proverbial money trough called an escrow account!

All land must be zoned by state law. Owners of that land have the right to protect their investment by ensuring that the politicians are not playing unfairly with unreasonable zoning changes or restrictions that attempt to zone a landowner out of business for political or personal reasons. Such political shenanigans that result in the devaluation of the land will result in court challenges. Now we have the Town's government defending a case that benefits a few people simply to settle old political scores or to curry votes in a particularly vocal section of the town. In a sense these politicians are using public money as though it were their own. Again, the public seemingly fails to understand that ownership of the land takes precedence over arguments that are based upon loss of view or suggestions for a better use of the land for the sole benefit of the residents. Too often people think that petitions and other such public outcries to governmental agencies are the answer to resolving disputes over land use. These agencies that provide approvals for land development must follow the law and as quasi-judicial bodies must do what is best in the interest of *all* the people and the developer. The owner of the vacant land next to the land your home is on has a right to develop his parcel in the same or similar manner. It's not a matter of who came first! It's a matter of law and of parity!

Failure to accept this is sheer folly. Too many residents act emotionally and throw themselves into legal entanglements with all too willing lawyers, who guarantee nothing, but request a retainer and payment in a timely fashion in order to continue the case. In the end result, if the developer has dotted his I's and crossed his T's, the residents and/or the town will lose in court, no matter how long it takes. What is most repugnant about this entire process are the actions of the politicians who patronize the public and get away with it. The politicians' con begins with him/her taking the residents' side of a disagreement while knowing full well that the position of the residents is in direct opposition to the law. In fact, the politician may visit the neighborhood and have meetings, and the residents think that they are on the inside track as to what is happening in Town Hall. This may go on for several months and one can observe the body language at public meetings between that politician and the members of the group. Often times sub-rosa conversations may occur in the halls or outside the building. What does all this accomplish? Well, when the public loses its battle, the politician can then blame the legal system, the courts and, of course, the lawyers, thus ingratiating him/herself with the unsuspecting public that has been duped by this disingenuous cad. How very pathetic! (This type of political ruse was so vividly played out by former Councilpersons Weber, Berry, Rapposelli and Davidson.)

One's home is a major investment. Families do not move to or invest in a dying community. People want naturally to be a part of a positive and enriching experience—something good and wholesome for themselves and for their children. People who move to suburbia want a current social address. Say what you will, disagree if you wish, but conventional wisdom dictates that Americans are upwardly mobile and suburbanites are the perfect example of this progression. Washington Township in Gloucester County is one South Jersey community that enables this progression by providing a diverse selection of homes at various price ranges. A premier address without premier prices! This community provides the perfect solution to the question of where to raise a family.

This type of planning doesn't occur by accident. It requires the mayor of a community to be proactive in seeking development that will enrich and support the wants and needs of the community. Failure to do this will result in higher taxes and the devaluation of property. Prior to 2001, this community was the richest in Gloucester County in tax ratables and yet was not the highest in property taxes. The community received outstanding public services and boasted superior pubic schools. All this good was the result of a carefully orchestrated plan begun in 1986 and carried through until 2000. Regrettably the Davidson administration, which followed 12 years of creative and innovative leadership, was an abysmal failure. This administration closed the town's doors to commercial/light industrial growth by putting politics before the people. Taxes were raised and services diminished! The mayor and Council seated in 2001 has placed the town in reverse gear. Unfortunately for the people, this backslide into a pre-1985 mindset embraced intimidation and the corruption of power within the government, serving only the chosen few. The appointment of politically driven and sometimes incompetent department heads crushed the morale of the employees, the enthusiasm of the people and the spirit of innovation, creativeness and enterprise. The cohesive fiber that once made this community one in spirit and put the "town" in "township" has been abandoned for self-aggrandizement and personal agendas.

Does the average citizen ever pause to think about the reasons why a developer invests in a community? Well, after twelve years of being a mayor, I believe that I now have the answers to that question:

- It enables families to live the American Dream.

- It spurs the economy, provides jobs, and attracts other investors.

- It reflects the healthy financial stability of the community.

- It's a barometer as to the social and educational growth of a community,

- It increases property values and the gross aggregate of ratables.

The public, the politicians and the press blame developers for everything that is wrong with a community, which is myopic thinking on their part. What is really wrong is the myopic, shallow and unintelligent lack of understanding of economic growth by those groups and, regrettably, by the elected leaders of a town who are unable to muster the basic creativity to think outside the box. And in some cases the size of that box equates to a ring box!

I have come to know only a few elected officials in my tenure who realized the importance of economic growth. These people were willing to stand up and be counted when attacked and ridiculed by the uninformed and the misinformed. If not for them and the Planning Boards of the 1990's, this community would be anything but South Jersey's Premier Community. These men and women join the honor roll of leaders: John Robertson, Bill Haines (deceased), Len Simmons (deceased), John Rogale, Sam Hart, Agnes Gardiner, Jane Huesser John Sczcerbinski, and many other volunteers. In order to provide a developer, investor and real estate broker the confidence to invest in a community, you need leaders who are intelligent, resourceful, confident, competent and informed and who don't let personalities get in the way of voting what is right for a town. These leaders must be willing to stand against the ignorant and uninformed, subjecting themselves to unfair and unjustified criticism and attacks by the people and the press. In order to achieve the economic development in this community between 1985 and 2000, it took the boldest of steps, intelligence, courage and leadership. This unprecedented and consummate achievement eclipsed all of Gloucester County and the southern part of Camden County. In spite of the naysayers and voices of doom and gloom, the seeds planted by John Robertson flourished under my administration due to my attentiveness to the needs of the community. I appointed the first economic development team to my staff in 1989. With the commitment of Don Amodei, Peter Murraco and Eleanor McNamara to this challenge. These people developed a print and video package that was incredible and was responsible for attracting the bulk of businesses to the community that are still part of the landscape. Given all that this team did for economic development, which caused the Township to become ratable rich, they were nevertheless the target of public ridicule by

Councilpersons Bob Berry (deceased) and Mary Virginia Weber. As time passed, it became quite obvious that both of these elected officials suffered from a severe case of jealousy and envy, of which there is no known cure.

Given the hostile atmosphere created by Berry, Weber their political cronies—and their ally in the press, Maureen Graham—Amodei, Murraco and McNamara stepped aside at my request in order that the town could move ahead in the area of economic development. Councilperson Sam Hart was committed to economic development and agreed to head the first citizens-appointed board and the Economic Development Council (EDC) was formed. With his leadership, dedication and willingness to work hand in hand with the Mayor's Office, an alliance between the EDC and the Mayor's Office was effected and businesses came to the township in numbers, providing millions of dollars in tax revenue per year. The Premier Community was officially born. And now as we read the journals that forecast the future of economic development across America, specifically the Greater Northeast, we are dismayed when we read: "Washington Township's Golden Days of Economic Development came to a close in the early part of 2001 when the Township's Planning Board, Town Council and Mayor removed the sign, 'Washington Township Welcomes Your Business.'"

The Golden Years of economic development didn't come without a price. Rather than accede to the obvious success of the Economic Development Plan and giving the Mayor, Councilman Hart and the EDC unconditional support for this achievement, petty jealousies and political rancor set in. The diminutive minds of certain Councilpersons (Bob Berry, Genny Weber, Joe Yost, Matthew Lyons, Ray Rapposelli and Randee Davidson) and their duplicitous supporters seemingly would go to any means to ensure that all successful projects would be marred and tarnished in some fashion to negate the positive contributions to the town. Any developer working with the Mayor's Office in bringing commercial and light industrial ratables to the community would fall victim to these well-planned and carefully orchestrated character assassinations. Regrettably, the developer, and others and I who successfully worked on behalf of the residents in making this community a premier address, would systematically be antagonized by unscrupulous politicians, arrogant and uniformed residents and a reporter, Maureen Graham, who peddled groundless innuendo, half-truths, uncorroborated statements and undocumented information, all under the protection of the First Amendment.

Chapter 13

The Unholy Alliance

Previously, I addressed my respect of John Robertson. I may have not always agreed with him or his approach to problem solving, but he knew how to cut through the minutia of governmental rhetoric. He appointed department heads void of politics and directed them to stay out of politics and do their jobs. He appointed professionals to work with him and several appointed boards to ensure that the new government would step off on the right foot and stay the course. It would be impossible to correct many of the errors of the community's early leaders or to undo mistakes and shortcuts taken by several residential builders whose methods were suspect. There is no future in the past and Robertson realized that. It was a time for healing and a time to move forward. He was not blessed with the most intelligent or receptive Council, and once Council faced the reality of its diminished role in this new government, the tone of cooperation went sour!

As I discussed earlier, Council had the authority to introduce and pass ordinances and they reviewed and voted upon the Mayor's proposed budget and approved the bill list posted each month. They also held a nebulous right to vote on selected mayoral appointments under a section of the Administrative Code referred to as Advice and Consent. This poorly worded and ill-defined section of the Administrative Code crafted by a pseudo-intellectual attorney would be challenged for almost 15 years until it was finally resolved by New Jersey's Supreme Court in 2001. (The impetus for the Court's action was a result of a lawsuit, one of many that Council members Lyons, Rapposelli and Davidson would bring against me as Mayor or against the Township over a two-year period that challenged my right to make appointments and to pay employees regardless if the Council withheld their Advice and Consent. The Court ruled in my favor, saying that the Mayor, as the executive branch of the government, can make appointments and set salaries as long as the amounts stipulated for those salaries do not exceed the total budget previously approved by Council. This was one of many lawsuits filed and lost by the Township at a cost to the taxpayer.) It was obvious to the residents who took an interest in the new government that there was a pernicious underlying discord among the Council members and between the Council and the Mayor.

Early on in the new government, jousting at the Council meetings was commonplace. The question of nepotism arose when a Councilperson's family member was hired for a position. In the rush to counter anything that the mayor and the solicitor might do to further discussions on the matter and to resolve the appointment through the channels provided for by the State of New Jersey, Council moved to appoint a local Ethics Board. This board of local appointed citizens would be the guardian of honesty and integrity in government. The mechanics of it (the number of members who would serve, the process of appointing them, the scope of their authority) and the ultimate power of the board became a focus of many heated and raucous meetings. This was not going to be an easy task. As mentioned, the State of New Jersey already had such a committee in place and would eagerly respond to any complaint filed in the proper form and yet, Council was still determined to have its own Ethics Board and that mindset could not be reasoned with.

Council's shortsightedness was brought to task when the community began to ask questions regarding how to go about locating, appointing and ensuring the integrity and non-political nature of this board, and how to unequivocally determine that the appointees have no affiliation with any Council member or the Mayor? The community was dubious about the idea and believed that it would be impossible to develop such a committee that could do its duties in an impartial fashion. The attempt to create such a committee at the local level is fatuous! Most people felt that if the appointees lived in the community, they surely had opinions from what they read in the press or heard around town. Flying in the face of these objections and, most importantly in defiance of conventional wisdom, The Local Ethics Board was formed. As predicted by many insightful community members, the Local Ethics Board became the Local Complaints Board. And as further expected by the insightful, this Local Ethics Board was simply a vehicle to be utilized by the provocateurs to embarrass specific appointed or elected officials.

It didn't take long once the Local Ethics Board was in place that it began to entertain complaints from Councilman Richard Marsella (deceased) and Ginny Weber that Mayor Robertson's relationship with a local developer, Tom Hedenberg, was unhealthy and perhaps unethical. Hedenberg was Township born and raised and earned his money the hard way, by working for it. He was and still is an honest, hardworking no-nonsense man who took the necessary risks in order to realize financial gain. Developers like Hedenberg leverage a great deal of money, requiring them at times to put everything they own on the line before a project has seen a shovel in the ground. The process of bringing a project to fruition is a long and arduous task. Many individuals who think it is easy have tried and failed. So often the uninformed, the novices, are quick to attribute luck to a developer's success when, in fact, it's about courage, determination, fortitude, honesty, integrity and risk taking. And as many of you know, risk taking is an action that is quite foreign to the many who seek security!

Tom Hedenberg was a risk taker and a prudent man who to this day continues to plan, develop and deliver quality projects that have infused this community's wealth not just in dollars but architecturally and aesthetically. All successful, self-made individuals quickly develop enemies many of whom they have never met or interacted with. This is the human condition called envy and those who possess such a character flaw are lurking in the shadows waiting for the opportunity to attack, hoping to make what is good into injurious evil.

When politicians decide *to get someone* it's amazing how far they will go and with whom they will align themselves in order to affect the dastardly deed. When Councilpersons Marsella (D) and Weber (R) joined forces, along with several malcontents who saw the worst in everything and everyone, and a local reporter who thrived on *making* the news rather than *reporting* it, the necessary ingredients were in place to manufacture a scandal through the use of innuendo, half-truths, association and downright fabrication. Mayor Robertson's relationship with Tom Hedenberg was no secret. After all, they were friends and neither one denied that friendship, and frankly there was no reason to do so. The approvals that Hedenberg received from either the Planning Board or Zoning Board, according to my research, followed the usual and customary process with public hearings and careful scrutiny by the licensed professionals. This routine process was made to appear as though the members of the respected boards were somehow coerced or politically manipulated into granting approvals. Permits issued for construction or subsequent inspections were reported as suspicious or suspect and not following customary procedures. One reporter in particular began to run stories that strung together isolated and unrelated items, carefully integrating them with reports of Hedenberg's approvals from the various boards, comments from dubious or unnamed sources, statements purported as fact which could not be corroborated, and of course the insistent and ad nauseam references to the friendship between him and the Mayor. The unrelenting press was always sure to have opinions and comments from political adversaries such as Councilpersons Marsella and Weber which, in the opinion of many, were simply acrimonious. In the opinion of the informed and responsible, these two elected officials disregarded their fiduciary responsibilities in order to gain political advantage. Good government took a back seat to the circus atmosphere which they orchestrated for every public meeting. Their mission was to destroy John Robertson. Regrettably they were destroying the image of the community at the same time and they seemed not to care.

As with any political melee of this magnitude, any cogent and responsible statement made by Mayor Robertson or other responsible, informed and intelligent individual never received the same attention by the reporters and were usually omitted or abbreviated in the press article as to lessen their impact. After all, why confuse the issue with the facts when the fiction is more interesting and sells paper? Money is King and with the press, it's the fuel that drives the presses.

The Local Ethics Board was ill-equipped to handle this time bomb. Letters to the State's Attorney brought yet another unfortunate siege of adverse publicity upon the community. Regrettably the community was getting a bum rap and in many circles this beautiful town became a joke! In the end, with little or no fanfare, minimal press coverage and not one apology, it was determined by the State's Attorney that there was nothing improper, illegal or unethical in the relationship between Hedenberg and Mayor Robertson, nor was there anything improper on the town's behalf in any of the approvals, permits or inspections relative to Hedenberg's projects. These two men had their characters assassinated and their lives almost gratuitously made into a wasteland. Two honest and upright men and their families were victims of the ugly side of politics.

Hedenberg continues to develop outstanding projects in the community and is proud to call this town his home. Robertson chose not to run for reelection. Had I known that, my life would have been totally different! If only I'd had a crystal ball. Little did I know that my friends and I would at sometime in the future become the next victim for Mary Virginia "Ginny" Weber, her sidekick Bob Berry and their merry band of trouble-makers. Worse yet, a bigger storm loomed in the future with a new breed of character assassins in the likes of Matthew Lyons, Ray Rapposelli and Randee Davidson. And guess what? There was one constant through all of this and it was the same reporter that John Roberston confronted—*Maureen Graham.*

Chapter 14

A GOLDEN OPPORTUNITY LOST

Every one of us has kicked ourselves when we pass up an opportunity that may have benefited us. How many times have we heard the expression "opportunity knocks only once"? In politics, there are times when an opportunity presents itself that could benefit the residents but politicians seem to be blind to it. I can't pinpoint specifically why this myopia manifests itself more times in politicians than in any other judicial or quasi-judicial body. Perhaps it's that most politicians do not demonstrate much creativity or imagination. No, they tend to deal with the more obvious, mundane issues that they can easily handle with little effort and, if they play their cards right, can look great in the public's eye, especially if they are able to manipulate the press. The latter statement also describes lawyers who, for the most part, are not too creative. I would venture to say that at least 75% of lawyers are mediocre, and that is frightening. Too many lawyers get involved in politics and serve as elected officials. And also of grave concern is the fact that a few of these mediocre lawyers may come to represent or prosecute you someday, or even be that judge sitting on the bench. That thought really disturbs me!

Another reason why politicians miss the opportunity to seize an idea and to develop it into a significant program or useful contribution to the people is the lack of stamina. In order to develop an idea and to take it from concept to completion takes work. Any great idea requires behind-the-scenes work that usually goes virtually unnoticed until the very end. Many politicians can't see the benefits of investing too much time into any one project. No, they would rather have many smaller ideas or programs that I refer to as flash in the pans, hit and runs, what is trendy and where is the action. They are looking for anything that can garner them newsprint and a photo-op. They say that all press, whether good or bad, is good. In other words, the photo-op and the story are more important that what, if anything, is actually accomplished. I disagree.

Perhaps the least flattering and most repugnant action perceived by the public is the politician who is the jouster, (not to be confused with jester although similar in the final analysis). This politician's perception of why he/she was elected to public office was that it was a mandate, by the people, and that he/she must be the watchdog for the electorate. Talk about an inflated ego and a convoluted self-perception of one's purpose in life! This takes the prize. Worst of all, these self-appointed guardians of the people are usually the catalyst for initiating an argument at a meeting and then carefully extricating themselves from the fray. As if that weren't enough to be defined as a cad, they begin to mock the other officials or appointed professionals by making faces, rolling their eyes, playing to the audience in the hopes of eliciting laughter and of course, making rude, crude and very unflattering remarks as to others' intelligence, demeanor or ideas. How pathetic! This type of elected official is a disgrace and makes a mockery of the dignity and respect that is at the very core of the democratic process.

The final insult perpetrated by these asinine jousters upon the public and their colleagues is when they openly patronize the public. Members of the public perceive this as a validation of their position as they grasp the microphone to make sure their words are heard. The insincere official will pick up on what the resident is addressing and begin to insert words of support, encouragement, a few amens and a hallelujah or two. The resident and the official become symbiotic at some point, now arguing with the other elected officials, receiving applause and other overt gestures of support and approval. Of course the resident has been used as a vehicle for political advantage and perhaps a few good quotes in tomorrow's press. This inexcusable behavior can only be defined as the actions of an insincere, beguiling politician. And to add insult to injury, nothing has been accomplished. This was one of the ploys used so often by many of the politicians with whom I was subjected to over the years. Their names may not be important now, but these people deserve to be noted for the record; Councilpersons Bob Berry (deceased), Joe Yost, Matthew Lyons, Ray Rapposelli, Randee Davidson, and the prime dilettante, Ginny Weber.

In 1985 this Township had the opportunity to come together as one town and one address. They often say what is in a name? Well, its identity! This community is served by seven zip codes of which TWO are areas within Washington Township. The other five zip codes are of towns not within the Township. We are one of several Washington Townships in the state. My efforts and those of Mayor Robertson over a period of 16 years in attempting to change the position of the U.S. Postal Service in providing us one zip code has met with many explanations, but always a firm "NO." The sad part of all this is that the time to do something to rectify this loss of identity occurred in 1985, when the community had decided to change its form of government. These four golden years were lost to political theatrics, as explained in earlier chapters. Instead of joining with Mayor Robertson and cooperating with him in a show of unity to the people in working to solidify the town's identity, Council chose to play war games and other such tactical nonsense in order to advance their own political agenda and those of their respective political party. As each year passed, so did the Golden Opportunity for a change that would last a lifetime and serve many generations to come. Regrettably, too many of those elected officials could think no further ahead then to the next election. This same kind of short-range and politically motivated thinking was prevalent in 1999 when the trio of Lyons, Rappposelli and Davidson got voted into office. Under the heavy hand

and direction of Attorney Jack Trimble, these Councilpersons only thought about the next election, not the people.

Since the 1960's the town's leadership permitted residential developers to determine the geographical layout of Washington Township. These same developers also imposed a type of isolation by developing so many neighborhoods, each with its own unique name. People no longer identified themselves with a community name, but rather by a housing development's name. Who was doing the planning in this community? Who had a vision for this town's future? Worse yet, many of the areas of the Township developed by a few money-hungry residential builders between the years 1960 to 1982, had absolutely no imagination in planning. By design they overdeveloped many areas due to the small building lot requirements and further impacted these areas by failing to provide suitable green space, thus creating a social stratum that began to separate this community into the haves and the have nots. Additionally, the town fathers did not control the number of strip malls constructed, many of which will never be totally occupied due to location. Again, where were the planners?

This section of *The Mayor's Chronicles* would be incomplete without revisiting former Mayor Robertson's attempt to pursue the idea of ONE name, ONE town, ONE mailing address, ONE people. I was pleased to continue with this mission during my tenure. I came to realize early on in my tenure as mayor that changing the direction of the U.S. Postal Service is an insurmountable task. Once the Blackwood and Sewell post offices were expanded to their present size, the goal of one mailing address for the town all but evaporated. The amount of research, time, lobbying and effort that I put into this project was without boundaries. I took umbrage that the press gave my successor, Ms. Davidson, print on her efforts to do the same thing. It was quite obvious that she had plagiarized my work since I did leave all that information in the files. Mayor Randee Davidson's lame and ineffective effort on this project defined her entire term in office which, by all standards, was simply mediocre to poor.

The importance of identity is now a moot subject since the community, by its accomplishments, is quite well known throughout the region, the state and the East Coast. The impetus behind all this was simply to have an identity that would have permitted all its residents to have one mailing address, listings in one phone directory and the advantage of giving simple directions to moving companies, out-of-towners and delivery companies. I was always so proud of the Township that I became insulted when the Washington Lake Park, the Center for the Performing Arts, the WTAA complex or our magnificent high school complex was advertised as being in Sewell, N.J., when in fact the town of Sewell is in Mantua Township.

All this confusion over a name! Amazing isn't it? The Postal Service told me that moving the mail in an expedient manner takes precedent over a community's need to have an identity. If the Township Committees of earlier times had taken action, this situation would have been resolved before the decade of the 1980's. The history of the community provided a legacy of names in Grenloch, Bunker Hill, Hurffville,

Chapel Heights, Turnersville and others. Council in the mid-1980's decided to make it a ballot issue that included a school project of Name the Town. Contributions from the general public and the school children favored names of the developments in which they lived because this is how so many people identified where they lived. In the opinion of many folks, we didn't need to inflate the ego of one particular developer, Joseph Esposito, whose impact on this community as to the number of residential units constructed is unmatched to this day and who attempts to claim sire rights for the Township (using the archaic definition of *sire* found in the Random House Dictionary). The conscious decision not to name anything remotely connected with Esposito was a wise one. The ballot question produced too many choices, with no clear-cut winner. This exercise may have been politically correct, but was more divisive then conciliatory. If Council went with the name that actually won on the ballot question, school children would have been insulted, residents would have cried foul and the public would have perceived this exercise as perfunctory and patronizing. This was a no-win situation and politicians never want to find themselves in a situation from which they cannot extricate themselves with dignity.

Washington Township is uniquely politically charged. Some tell me it's because so many of its residents come from the rough-and-tumble politics of Philadelphia. Although having been involved in the community since 1969, I would grant credence to that statement. I do question, however, why some people who get involved in the political process are so mean-spirited. As to the Council members, some of them simply

never got the idea as to how this form of government func-
tioned. Their inability to understand and accept their role as
Councilpersons as specifically outlined in the Administrative Code is a steady source of internal strife and public rancor. These egos, paired with the agendas of many other
individuals in the community, would set the stage for many
unnecessary conflicts that would repeatedly strike at the very
heart of this town. Over the years it became abundantly clear
to me that many residents who would attend Township meetings had a wanton disrespect for the rights of others and had
absolutely no understanding of fair play, honesty, and integrity in addressing the issues. To many, it was a badge of
courage to get something over another person or to blindside
them, ambush them or create minefields for others to maneuver. This was the calling card of many residents and far
too many Councilpersons.

In the final analysis, the overwhelming majority of people
in a community choose not to get involved in politics. For
those people who may have considered it, the actions of a
few are found to be so reprehensible, so obnoxious and so
horrific as to deter them from making a move that would
place them in harm's way and perhaps make them the next
target of these profane individuals. When this kind of community malaise sets in, it opens the door for others whose
agendas may be suspect, motives self-serving and commitment to serving the people less than honorable!

Part II

THE ARDUOUS TIMES

THROUGH ADVERSITY WE CREATE OPPORTUNITIES

INTRODUCTION

Part II of *The Mayor's Chronicles* will focus specifically on my three terms as Mayor, beginning in January of 1989 through December 31, 2000. Also, I will address my term as a State Assemblyman and the period ending with the conclusion of this book in the Spring of 2004.

As with any book of this nature, it is essential for me to focus on several situations, problems and other occurrences that marked my administration's 12 years of service to the community and to highlight what I feel to be the many successes that contributed in making Washington Township a Premier Community.

This section of the book will also deal with the effective problem-solving methods that were implemented to reach equitable, fair and beneficial resolve in a period of time that saw Washington Township blossom into the flower of Southern New Jersey. It will become obvious that through a dedicated and committed team under my leadership, Washington Township took its rightful place as South Jersey's number-one community. Economic growth reached its apex and the control of residential growth increased the value of all property, while the market for new and resale homes commanded the highest prices in the area WITHOUT major increases in property taxes. In fact, the Township's tax rate was one of the lower in the entire County, which includes 24 communities. Many residents as well as observers in the county and the state refer to this period of leadership as "The Golden Years."

It will be necessary to focus on the not so pleasant situations that at times raised their ugly heads. I will focus on several of these situations in order to address what their potential could have been in dividing neighborhoods and pitting resident against resident. Many of these situations were politically motivated by those charged with the responsibility of leading this community. The agenda of these politicos and their cohorts was to undermine and to cause irreparable damage to the *esprit de corps* that my administration had successfully built in bringing a fragmented community together. It was also necessary to address the issue of low morale among the employees. With the careful selection of department heads, fairly negotiated contracts, respectable salaries and an excellent benefits package, we accomplished excellent working conditions and a family atmosphere. In the words of former Senator John Matheussen (R-4th District/NJ), "Jerry Luongo put the Town in Township."

Highlighting problems may seem incongruous with enumerating successes. It's my belief, however, that sharing problems and their solutions serves five basic purposes:

- To vividly demonstrate what people can do when working cohesively in pursuing a common goal.

- To prove the axiom that no matter what you do, you can never please everyone.

- To expose politicians and their cronies for the pain that they inflicted on certain employees, depriving them of jobs, maligning their good names and causing emotional trauma to the individuals and their families.

- To try to comprehend the unreasonable, uncompromising and, at times, borderline psychotic behavior of certain residents towards neighborhood problems, my administration and me.

Some readers may feel that I am setting the stage in order to attack people on a personal level. To that, my response is simple: if you wrote or said something in public or you did something in private that has been documented and corroborated by another individual, I will hold you accountable and let the public evaluate you. After all, many unkind things were done to me and my friends, so I am simply subscribing to the intent of the old adage, "What goes around comes around." Other readers, however, may conclude that this book is a platform for me to make assertions, draw conclusions or offer hypotheses about events, relationships and decisions which may be incorrect. Based upon the plethora of information that I have in print and on tape recordings, I will stand by my statements and will also state that I am right on target. A few readers may say, "Who cares about what you have to say?" My response is somewhat philosophical in nature and tends to be humanitarian at its core: if only one person who was attacked by the venomous political cliques that exist in this community is vindicated and redeemed, I have succeeded in my mission. I feel confident in stating that in my years of community service, I have never knowingly or with premeditation ever hurt anyone. With that admission I will record, as objectively as possible, what I experienced as Mayor and Assemblyman, basing my observations and statements on the assertion that politics is not a license or mitigation for corrupt and contemptuous behavior. I further submit that when the public fails to reject such behavior as unacceptable, its silence implies acceptance and validation. When this occurs, negativity begins to escalate exponentially and can be the one element, if permitted to fester unabated, which will surely destroy the cohesive fiber of a community. Once this level of apathy consumes a community, the political vultures will swoop down, feeding upon the people's perception of despair, doom and gloom.

The perfect example of this can be found in many New Jersey cities. Politicians promised a utopia but took the best and left the rest. Be wary of those politicians unable to focus or discuss issues in a civilized, intelligent and coherent fashion. Usually behind that mask of compassion and understanding is a nefarious character. Our community and county seemingly have had a disproportionate number of this breed of onerous politicians and individuals in the service of the public!

As to Washington Township and Gloucester County, I will in Part II cite specific instances and individuals who, in my opinion from firsthand and very unpleasant experiences, will do anything in order to promote themselves in the political ranks, regardless of the cost to their integrity, character and morality. In many of these instances, these unscrupulous individuals personify to the highest degree all that is wrong with politics. These kinds of errant men and women represent the dark side of politics. You as the reader can judge for yourself.

When I decided that I would comment on the behavior of individuals who have interfaced directly in my life and, at times, affecting it in a negative fashion, I felt it important to implement many of the skills that I learned in psychology and sociology while in pursuit of a Ph.D. It was essential to be as objective as possible, and given the nature of the political beast, that is rather difficult. Therefore, using the categories of overt behavior manifested by parents and siblings in family counseling, I felt comfortable in categorizing the people who I will write about in this section of the book. The five categories of overt behavior to be researched in family counseling was my guide:

1. **Simple fool:** opens his/her mind to any passing thought, lacks discernment and will do anything he/she is told just to be part of the group. No sense of loyalty or self-respect.

2. **Silly fool:** basically thick-headed, stupid; responds in anger and usually his mouth gets him/her into trouble. If he/she kept his/her mouth closed, he/she would improve people's opinion of him/her.

3. **Sensual fool:** rejects common decency and is only interested in meeting his/her immediate goal without think-

ing about cause and effect of his actions. He/she has a bent for making wrong choices.

4. **Scoring fool:** one who uses facial expressions and other types of physical gestures to show his/her abhorrence and repugnance towards people and ideas which contradict his/her erroneous conclusions and convoluted ideas. He/she expresses scorn through derisive attitudes and behaviors as well as in speech.

5. **Steadfast fool:** an individual who is self-confident and close-minded. He/she is committed to him/herself and cares about no one else. He/she will do all possible to enlist others to join him/her in hurting others. Usually this person preys on weak-minded people who can be manipulated. Also a master of the lie.

(*Principles of Family Counseling.* Advanced Training Institute of America. c. 1995. Used with permission).

Chapter 15

PIGS AND TRASH

This is not a very pleasant subject for dinner conversation, but it's a situation that was never addressed properly by an entire group of elected officials. Either by their personal and financial investment, friendships or involvement as contractors of record, several large parcels of land sold to housing developers were never properly prepared for residential building. It would be years before this problem surfaced, creating an almost catastrophically negative effect on property values, home-resale values, the Township's image and the reputation of several former elected and respected officials. Their questionable and unethical business practices, and their relationships with a major national home construction company whose stock was traded on the New York Stock Exchange, would be called into question.

I inherited this problem when I became Mayor, being blindsided by the information at a public meeting by a Councilman. Unfair you ask? You bet! Unethical? Absolutely! Politically motivated? Of course! This problem that predated my administration by almost ten years had now become my responsibility, and to the dismay of my adversaries and to the gratitude of the residents, I would solve the problem!

The historical perspective on this matter needs to be revisited in order for readers to understand for themselves how situations such as this are permitted to happen. The question of culpability presented itself when the Township developed a plan to address the matter, but had yet to implement that plan to the fullest in order to achieve the anticipated results. Pig farming is still a part of the "real Sewell's" economy. (Note the use of the "real Sewell"—the mailing address for majority of Washington Township residents, although these residents DO NOT LIVE in Sewell. It's just a post office that sorts and delivers their mail and nothing more.) Now we will talk about pigs and how these little porkers came to play a role in one of several calamitous events that would unfold over the years.

At one time, several farmers in Washington Township raised pigs. That business evaporated in the early 1960's and is no longer a concern. The smell of a pig farm carries well beyond the property line. Unless you are a pig farmer, you would probably find the odor less than refreshing. Pig farming can be quite profitable, especially if you can feed those short-legged, cloven-hoofed, bristly-hair and blunt-snout mammals garbage. And the profitable way to get garbage is to use your property as a landfill or dump. The hill that lies behind the Five Points Diner at the intersection of Routes 47 and 41 is a landfill. Once flat farmland, it grew exponentially as Deptford Township became a dump for many neighboring communities and area cities. Due to the leadership efforts of a community advocate, Mrs. Bea Cerkez—who would later be elected to Deptford Township Committee serving as Mayor for many years—the landfill was closed, covered and continues to be monitored until this day.

The Deptford Township landfill can be seen and sometimes smelled for a distance. In fact, considering the landfills in Pine Hill, Gloucester Township and Monroe Township, this section of South Jersey was the cities' and small towns' dump for many years. Money was made by the owners of these dumps and the environmental impact on these sites would affect the ecological balance of our lands and watersheds for many decades.

However, the worst offenders of this large-scale, irresponsible and unabated dumping were the pig farmers. At least three of these pig farmers were in Washington Township. Of course their names are part of the urban legend that the history of Washington Township characterizes as "saddened when the builders' bulldozers began to rape this beautiful land." That sadness was short lived as those farmers collected their respective checks from the very developers they characterized as the "rapists." To put it bluntly, those farmers cried all the way to the bank!

These pig farmers accepted garbage trucks from as far west as Philadelphia. When the truck arrived, they systematically dumped their loads as often as seven days a week. The farmer would then separate, to the degree possible, the garbage from the trash and then feed the garbage to the pigs. To dispose of the trash, the uneaten garbage and the pig manure, the farmer dug pits and buried all this without any type of treatment whatsoever. To disguise the obvious, these dumps were seeded, giving the illusion that nothing more than green fields existed, when in fact a chemical reaction was developing under tons of soil. It was methane, an odorless, colorless, flammable gas (CH_4), the major constituent of natural gas which is used as a fuel and an important by-product of organic compounds. Given the years of dumping and the extent of burying, there was a massive area of decomposition of the constituents that create methane gas under what was to be a site of a major housing subdivision.

At some undefined period in time, probably the late 1950's, the dumping ceased, the pigs disappeared and the burying desisted. The land sat dormant for a period of time and was finally purchased in the early 1970's by the Orleans Corporation, a respected builder of custom homes, condominiums, multi-residential units and commercial sites. The corporation continues to do business in the Township and surrounding areas and has an excellent reputation. Unlike several other builders who came to Washington Township, built their homes, sold them and then filed for bankruptcy, leaving residents and township officials with numerous problems to deal with, the Orleans Corporation has taken pride in its family name, standing behind its product.

The Orleans Project was presented to the Planning Board, received approvals that would extend into the late 1980's, secured building permits and subsequently began construction of several hundred homes, creating another community neighborhood. In researching the records that remain from those Planning Board sessions, I was chagrined to find *not one single question* was ever asked by the Board or the public with regard to the previous use of the property as a dump and pig farm. It would be discovered later on that several officials, residents and even an attorney knew of the land's prior use, but chose to remain silent!

In the early part of the 1990, residents began complaining to my office about digging up trash when installing fences, sheds, additions and in-ground pools. The residents came to a Council meeting to address their concerns. At that meeting Councilman Leonard Simmons (deceased) made a statement that simply dumbfounded everyone when he said, "Well, that's the site of the old Weatherby dump and pig farm." Any response at that time would be inappropriate. Although the information was scant, the press nevertheless had a field day with this information, totally disregarding the negative impact that such incomplete reporting would have on the homeowners and their major investment.

Within a day of that news story, the Mayor's Office phone and my home phone received a stream of calls. The residents wanted to know what would be done. As Mayor I was expected to respond, and rightfully so. I had nothing to do with any aspect of the project but the residents in the time of a crisis need a person or a place to turn and, in this situation, the Mayor was that person. It was essential that everything that was to be done relative to this situation be done in an orderly fashion. The first thing to do was to call a meeting of the neighborhood community and establish a dialogue. Fliers were hand-delivered to every resident's home announcing a meeting at the neighboring Chestnut Ridge Middle School. I knew that it was essential to be prepared with answers, to the degree possible, even though I was not familiar with the problem or the history of the property. I quickly assembled a team consisting of the Township Engineer and solicitor, representatives from the Delaware Valley Planning Commission, and the Township's Environmental Commission. I also urged Council members to attend and reached out to the Orleans Corporation to send a representative or to provide me with documentation as to any action they took in remediation of the land or that would support their due diligence in addressing the dump and the pig farm prior to construction. Records from the Planning Board and from the construction office relative to this project were gathered together and carefully reviewed to determine the Township's role in this entire situation.

Sometime over the weekend following the story about the trash and pigs in the newspaper, a mysterious brown envelope was discovered at my front door at my home. In it I found photos of the site, identifiable hauler's trucks filled with debris, and backhoes and bulldozers apparently in the process of burying the trash. Someone in this community had this information but never came forth when a resolution to the problem could have been effected BEFORE construction of the homes. Rather, the person or persons yet to be named dropped this matter into my lap. After consultation with the Township Attorney Joseph Alacqua, I was advised to consider appointing a Special Counsel, as lawsuits were inevitable. My first choice was then a good friend and my appointee to the Municipal Court of the Township, Bruce Hasbrouck of Woodbury, New Jersey. He had to decline the offer since he was representing a firm that had or was doing business with the Orleans Corporation at some point whether before or after the construction period. Calls to two other Gloucester County attorneys yielded the same result, "conflicts of interest." I then realized that I was about to open Pandora's Box!

The special team that I had assembled met, and with the help of aerial photos from over a 35-year period provided by the Delaware Planning Commission, it was obvious that there was extensive dumping, burying, earthmoving, apparently some removal of debris and finally a period of non-use that provided nature the time for the seeded areas to grow. Township records produced very little and it was questionable whether any inspections were ever made and if indeed any permits for dumping were ever issued to the Weatherby farm. I was now prepared to meet with the residents and to face their questions. Subsequent meetings would need to be scheduled to discuss progress, findings and finally, a master plan of remediation. I would need to accept the responsibility in bringing this matter to closure in a timely and orderly fashion, ensuring the integrity and value of the residents' homes.

As anticipated, the first meeting was tense. More questions than answers. Questions related to health, safety, integrity of the structures, property values and specifically, what was going to be done and when. All these concerns were appropriate and I understood what needed to be done. The Township had a responsibility to take decisive action and a moral obligation to the people. There was no passing of the buck, not even to the Orleans Corporation!

I discussed with Council the projected costs of such a resident-friendly plan and I addressed the fact that the statute of limitations precluded anyone being held accountable through litigation against those directly responsible for this travesty. Knowing that the residents wanted a commitment from the Township, I developed a plan and put it into writing. It was distributed to every homeowner in the development, since at this point no one really knew how many homes were affected. Specific sites could only be determined upon completion of an aggressive engineering study.

The plan was subject specific and addressed the following points with my promise and my word that the problem would be resolved:

1. The Township engineers, with the assistance of the Delaware Valley Planning Commission and an Environmental Engineering firm, would inspect the entire site, taking earth samples, testing ground water and installing monitoring wells to determine the scope of the contamination.

2. Once a map was drawn identifying the areas of contamination relative to trash, pig manure, methane gas and any other contaminants, a general homeowners meeting would be held to share all information.

3. Residents who chose to seek private counsel were encouraged to have their legal representative attend the general meetings. I further assured the residents that nothing would be held back and that all information would be shared, regardless of the Township placing itself in harm's way as to possible litigation. The Orleans Corporation agreed to be present, with its counsel, at every meeting held.

4. I informed Council that I had authorized the payment for all testing in order to expedite the process, although in all my meetings with the Orleans Corporation I stressed, without equivocating, that they should be totally responsible for all costs. The Orleans Corporation never said, "no," but refused to make any commitments until they saw the final report and exhausted all available avenues of any legal action against those contractors responsible for removing the waste.

5. Three such general meetings with all interested residents were planned. Fliers indicating pertinent information and an agenda were distributed to all residents. The meetings were conducted by me and the professionals addressing specific aspects of the overall remediation plan. The professionals answered each and every question as

directly as possible in terms easily understood to the layman.

6. A final plan was then developed that enumerated the affected properties, open space and public areas that were deemed contaminated. Rather than opt for the higher end on the scale of permissible contaminants as determined by the State of New Jersey and the federal government, I instructed the professionals to work in the lower end of the scale ensuring, to the degree possible, that this administration sought ZERO tolerance in leaving behind any contaminants if at all possible. (I was criticized by Township Council in taking that position. I felt strongly about my position and the arguments presented on that behalf were firmly rooted in empirical studies. Council's thinking was obtuse and frankly, empty-headed. The reason for my position was predicated of the knowledge that the EPA can change positions, rules and regulations relative to contaminants as to what is acceptable and what is not acceptable sometimes without rhyme or reason. I was not willing to put at risk the health and safety of the residents or the investment that they had in their properties.)

7. All homeowners whose properties were affected were notified by the Township's engineer, given the plan of remediation for their property, a timeline and a direct phone number for the professional assigned to their home. Calls were welcomed with no restrictions.

8. All homeowners were informed about the placement of monitoring wells, the scope of unearthing that would remove the contaminants, how the area would be restored and a timeline. Again, area newsletters written by me were distributed to the homeowners on a regular basis with updates as they became available.

9. The Mayor's Office agreed to provide a certified statement to any owner requesting same that the residential property site was free of all contaminants and that the property was deemed "clean." To my knowledge, not one home sold below market value based upon sales of homes within the Township on a comparable basis.

10. All lawsuits were settled by the Orleans Corporation. The Orleans Corporation also agreed to reimburse the township up to 50% of the total cost of the plan and the subsequent remediation. The total price tag for this project was $550,000.00. The Township absorbed its portion of $225,000.00 without a tax increase to the people. *Operation Clean-up was a success!*

As in any problem resolved successfully, a postscript is essential. I chose not to share with the press the contents of that mysterious brown envelope that was left at my door that included photographs, copies of the bills of lading that were altered to reflect more trash being removed from the property than what was actually removed, and the names of those individuals responsible for all this. I chose not to pursue these individuals for several reasons:

1. The statute of limitation had expired and therefore the Township could not recoup from these individuals any part of the $225,000 expended on the Township's part.

2. To simply expose these individuals and/or their company, all of whom were and still are residents of the Township, would only hurt their families, serving no useful purpose other than retribution and that reason is patently immoral in my opinion.

3. The only reason for such a negative action could only be considered political and this problem had nothing to do with politics.

4. I never subscribed to finger-pointing and I wasn't about to begin now. Although these contractors failed to perform due diligence, to blame these individuals totally when there were ample opportunities for the Township to discover all this prior to construction didn't seem equitable.

The Mayor needs to stand on his own two feet, not looking for a scapegoat to shoulder the blame or the responsibility of the position. Regrettably for the residents of this Township, the administration that took charge of this community in 2001 subscribed to finger-pointing, finding scapegoats for their incompetence, political retribution and outright lying.

Finally, no accounting of this episode in the Township's life would be complete without addressing the lack of leadership demonstrated by certain individuals who could have taken a proactive role in helping to resolve the problem. It was too bad that Councilpersons Robert Berry and Ginny Weber were so politically motivated as to try to undermine what was right for the people. These two Councilpersons attended most of the general homeowners meetings but kept to the back of the room, never offering even one comment, constructive or otherwise. As politics would have it with these two very difficult individuals, during the next campaign season when I sought a second term as Mayor, these two individuals and their cronies walked the affected residential development, passing out literature attempting to blame the entire situation on me. To the credit of the good people of this community, Berry, Weber and their cronies were run out of the development on a rail—and rightfully so!

Chapter 16

SINK HOLES AND BURIED TREASURE

So often, just when you think that the problems of the past will never again rear their ugly heads, think again! Even now in 2003, I marvel at how many residential builders prominent in the building boom years from 1965 to 1985 got away with so very much. Where were the planning boards, building inspectors and zoning officers? How could so many housing units be approved without appropriate permits or certificates of occupancy? Did the Township engineers during that period of time ever provide a comprehensive and extensive inspection of the common areas that would become the responsibility of the Township? I soon came to learn and understand that there were no real answers, just more questions. Questions that no one seemingly wanted to answer or, if answered, the answers fell short of exposing the culprits. It seemed as though once again, my administration would need to address more problems head on and without the benefit of complete files and reports. And in some cases, I was able to identify the residential builders by name, but regrettably the corporations formed to develop certain tracts of land had been dissolved and/or the statute of limitations had expired so they walked away with their money, leaving the community with their problems to remedy.

Previously I addressed the fact that the environmental agencies whose job it is to ensure the protection of the numerous natural resources often revisit policies, procedures, laws and mandates. Too often in my opinion, they jump to conclusions that create panic among the public and then, with a somewhat cavalier attitude, reverse their position, sometimes for the better, sometimes for the worse. In their defense, however, I'm sure that after further investigation, research and education, precise methods of measuring contaminants and determining their effect can warrant a change in posture which is deemed appropriate if not necessary.

For years, the approved and legal method for the disposing of building materials or items as a result of excavating and land clearing preparation for building, was burial. Given today's standards, the idea of burying building materials sounds so irresponsible. However, realizing the potential for problems, there were rigid standards in place. Obviously if the burying process were not properly implemented there could be serious problems caused by decomposition. Among the rules in place from 1960 through the early 1980's was that debris could not be buried under foundations, basement floors, slabs, driveways, public roadways or open space that was to be deeded to the township. No combustible materials or certain chemicals could be buried, but rather had to be taken to a landfill or other approved site. By what I have stated above, it is obvious that the front and rear yards would become the sites of all burying, which was restricted to only the materials from that specific unit. The materials needed to be broken down into small pieces to mix easily with clean fill dirt and therefore create a solid mass, eliminating the potential for sink holes caused by loosely compacted debris that decomposes. What needs to be reiterated here is the specificity of the regulations: only materials from the specific project could be buried on that site and no cans or containers containing any contaminants were permitted to be buried. In theory the State's plan seemed reasonable. In practice however, it was totally abused, improperly supervised and far from successful in many of New Jersey's communities and many other towns across the country. This law was a bonanza for the builders since the cost of carting and disposing of building materials and land-clearing debris offsite was costly and time consuming. For the most part, even restricted items found their way into the burying pits as well as materials from other building sites and other contractors. Who would ever know? Many of these burying sites produced revenue for unscrupulous builders who charged smaller companies for the service of burying their debris. No one was apparently watching or inspecting these sites as we would come to find out long after the project was completed and/or the developer left town or went bankrupt.

It was apparent that the developers/contractors on the job had no idea as to how Mother Nature would handle this invasion of her good earth. Dead trees, wood, plasterboard and sheathing will decompose. If not broken down and compacted with sufficient fill dirt, the decomposing process creates voids. Then the earth shifts and eventually depressions in the soil appear. These depressions begin to work outward until finally there is a collapse into what we know as sink holes. Sizes range from a small hole to ones capable of swallowing entire buildings and people. This kind of problem given the appropriate set of geological circumstances could be catastrophic. Many lives were lost in several New Jersey towns due to this problem.

The areas of the Township where this problem began to manifest itself were in Birches West, Twin Ponds East and the Spring Lake Developments. Three different developers/ builders—two of which have left the township and one who continues to call Washington Township home—seemed to be the apparent culprits in this improper burying of materials. By the calls received by the residents who saw the problem developing on their property, it was essential and quite prudent for my administration to be proactive and decisive. Although I believed that my administration was moving swiftly in addressing the problem, a few residents decided that the first call made should be to the press. When this happens, sensationalism and the selling of papers take precedence over good sense, logic and respect for the homeowners affected. Collectively there can be a decline in property values due to a stigma that is placed on the area. No one wins in this situation!

Given the challenge of yet another attack on the Township's integrity, the wheels of finding a solution were set into motion:

- To identify the scope of the problem.

- To identify areas in imminent danger to life or property.

- To initiate a comprehensive plan of remediation.

- To be mindful of property values and the negative affect on homeowners.

- To develop a plan to having developers admit to their blunder and participate fully in sharing the costs for all remediation. (I always believed this to be a long shot at best, given the law regarding statutes of limitations and the dissolution of the original corporations.)

In the process of implementing this plan, it seemed to me we should also investigate the open-space and recreational sites deeded to the Township by the developers. In my opinion, for someone who wanted to bury illegally or improperly, these areas would be prime locations.

Within days of discovering the first sinkholes, the Mayor's Office was inundated with calls from residents who had concerns. Names and addresses were carefully logged into a journal and a geological engineering firm was contracted to work with the Township's engineers in developing a process to address the problem. It was determined that a comprehensive plan in the use of a sophisticated sonar device would be used, which apparently could determine the extent of voids beneath the ground cover. Once again the services of the Delaware Valley Planning Commission were called in to review their file of aerial photographs taken of the entire area from 1960. These photographs proved to be an invaluable resource for locating the burying pits. Once an area was determined to be suspect, sonar was used to pinpoint the problem area, then drilling was executed. These exploratory drill sites would reveal if in fact a burying site was present and disclose what type of materials were buried there. If required, the site was excavated and the materials removed and disposed of properly at licensed landfills or transfer stations. The remaining dirt was sifted and clean additional fill dirt brought to the site. The excavation area was then filled, compacted and seeded. All materials from the site were identified, catalogued and an effort was made to determine the approximate time period that the materials were buried. This process was utilized on public as well as private lands. Any damage to private property was repaired and there was no cost to the homeowners. The success rate of this project was 98% effective.

To further exacerbate this problem, elevating it to a critical status, was the report of an easement collapse. In fact, five children were hurt due to the improper backfilling of sewer and water lines at a clean-out or gate-valve box. In these three same developments, collapses and sink holes around manhole covers in the streets played havoc with front-end alignments of those drivers who hit the bull's-eye. All these problems were discovered to be caused by improper workmanship—improper or illegal burying of materials—tied directly to the contractor of record. Given the number of hours billed to the contractor's escrow accounts by the professionals responsible for inspections, I have yet to understand how these people ignored or could not see what was being done in the field and not putting a stop to it. Furthermore, these professionals would need to recommend to Council the release of performance and maintenance bonds, two very critical forms of a financial obligation that provided a method for the Township to guarantee that all work was performed accordingly and in a timely fashion. If not, repairs would be at the contractor's cost, not the taxpayers. (As I studied the process over the years, carefully observing Council, members of the Zoning Board, Planning Board, the inspectors, and the professionals, I came to understand that certain developers simply skated through the process over the years. However, if you were a developer and thought to be supportive of the Mayor, everything that you did was inspected many times and permits and approvals for projects were slow in coming. Frankly, knowing the Mayor became a liability and that was unfair. The truth be told, some of the best projects in Washington Township were developed by "friends of the Mayor" and I take pride in knowing these people of honesty, character and integrity. Several public officials could learn a lesson about honesty, character and integrity by taking a page from the books of these individuals who conducted themselves and their businesses in a professional fashion, regardless of how ignorant members of the Zoning Board, Planning Board, the Council, the people and the press treated them.)

It never fails, there is always someone out there who always knows the full story behind a problem and chooses to remain silent, for whatever reason, permitting these dastardly acts of contractor's shortcuts to go unabated or undiscovered until they surface as a major concern. Within days of the stories about the illegal burying finding their way into the press, former employees of two of the developers contacted my office and wanted to tell me the truth about their bosses. They admitted that they were directly involved on the construction sites and without hesitation admitted that were told to bury building materials as well as anything else on the site as quickly and as cheaply as possible. "Dig a hole, bulldoze the materials in to it, cover with some top soil, seed and forget it" seemed to be the directions that were followed. As to following the rules and regulations, nobody gave a damn. Given the trash that was unearthed on these sites during the Township's cleanup operation "Buried Treasure," office papers, documents, bills and other office trash was found that proved that contractors from other sites and other towns were also burying on these sites. I suppose that they didn't shred their documents because they didn't think we would ever find out what they did. We passed inspections and that was all that they cared about. The informants were telling the truth. But once again, the law was on the side of the guilty. In attempting to pursue action against these developers, I was told that due to the Township's professionals signing off on inspections and both performance and maintenance bonds, I wouldn't have much of a case if I did get to court, let alone taking the risk of having the case thrown out before it even got before a jury. To spend the taxpayer's money in this fashion is patently wrong especially when there is no light at the end of the tunnel.

At this point I knew the identities of the culprits and even if they subcontracted this phase of their operation, they were ultimately responsible. Second, I always did my own research—not because I doubted the integrity of those responsible for such record keeping but because I had to answer to the people and I had to be unequivocally positive of the facts. Third, you can always be assured that a Councilperson will attempt to lay blame on the Mayor through innuendo or outright lies by initiating rumors that the Mayor is somehow involved with developers. I also knew of one reporter who would print just about anything negative, absent of facts or credible information as long as she could refer to an "unnamed source." Given the abuse of this whistle-blower's protection, one really begins to wonder if indeed the source is not the reporter him/herself simply regurgitating gossip. (I fully understand the need for this kind of protection in a high-profile case wherein fact, the life of an individual or his family would be imperiled. However, in politics this type of threat is very remote. Predicated upon that argument, this is where the abuse of the unnamed-source protection rule lies. If someone hasn't the courage to stand by the information which they provide and is not able to present incontrovertible facts to substantiate their claim, it should be viewed as *suspect*, especially when the person providing that information refuses to divulge his name or only speaks under the promise of anonymity. Every American has the right to face and question their accuser so states the VI Amendment to the Constitution. The press and the government seem to violate that Amendment, and no one but the aggrieved seems to care.)

Throughout New Jersey in areas that experienced rapid suburban growth, the problem of sinkholes and buried trash was an increasing concern. I attended two seminars as a panelist sponsored by the Environmental Protection Agency in Trenton. The horror stories conveyed by other New Jersey Mayors and the emotional testimony from residents were truly a frightening wake-up call. Complete streets, homes and recreational areas being swallowed by massive cave-ins. In some instances there were loss of lives and severe injuries. I knew that I must take decisive action!

Knowing from previous encounters that the developers were less than cordial, I knew that any dealings with Alan Cutler; the Costanzos, father and son; and Joe Esposito would be contentious at best. My investigation of this entire situation discovered that Cutler needed to deed open space to the Township before his maintenance bond was released. The Costanzos' maintenance bond was still in effect. Esposito's bonds had long been released and the construction company was no longer doing business and/or had declared bankruptcy. With this information in hand, I reached out to these three builders. Esposito, who built more housing units to the acre with the highest density in the Township, flat-out refused to do anything, blaming subcontractors and lamenting numerous personal financial problems. I knew Esposito through the Sons of Italy—John Facenda Lodge and believed that I had a reasonable relationship with him. (Many blamed Esposito for the failure of the Lodge due to his insistence in building a hall that far exceeded our needs and one that the Lodge could not afford. Esposito is first and foremost a businessman and the use of the Sons of Italy enabled him to get a much needed zoning approval and financial support for the building, which is the location of the Renaissance Room on Fries Mill Road. The building and subsequent legal problems with the New Jersey Alcohol and Beverage Control Agency divided the Lodge and its members, causing a major splinter group. Finally, the Lodge was forced to surrender its Charter. It was a sad day for all Italian-Americans who believed that the understanding of one's ethnicity and the history of one's roots is vital to understanding who we are as a people. Also the community lost a very vital community and charitable organization whose members gave quite generously from their hearts to those in need.)

Esposito's vitriolic attitude spoke vividly to the fact that he would make absolutely no concession or financial consideration in admitting wrongdoing. Cutler agreed to some remedial work, but was quick to blame his construction supervisor, who was the person who informed me where the burying pits were located, for ordering the burying and permitting the illegal dumping. Father and Son Constanzo questioned the Township's engineering reports and requested an on-site walk-through of the development.

The Township's engineer, the Director of Municipal Services James McKeever, and I inspected the sites along with the Constanzos. The Constanzo meeting proved counter-productive since father and son would accept no responsibility, even when faced with the inferior workmanship that was obvious by the back-filling of water and sanitary sewer lines throughout the development. At that point it was obvious that it would be necessary to take legal action through the bonding company. Any further discussions with the Constanzos would yield nothing positive.

The Township has a responsibility to the residents to ensure the integrity of all land that it either approved as part of a dwelling unit or accepted as open space. The removal of all debris and the restoration of all tainted soil in the affected areas were effectively and efficiently completed by a licensed contractor, approved by the Department of Environmental Protection and under the careful inspection of McKeever. Given Cutler's cooperation and the successful action against the bonding company representing Constanzo construction, the Township's cost of this project was reduced from $385,000 to approximately $150,000. The integrity of all homeowners' property and all open-space had been restored. Once again however, the taxpayers were required to foot a portion of the bill for the problems left by residential developers and of course, the mistakes of past administrations and/or their employees.

(Politics are always a part of government and with that in mind, a few things should be said. James McKeever was, in my opinion, one of the finest Directors of Municipal Services that this community has ever had. During Council's budget discussions in the 1999-2000 year, Councilpersons Lyons, Rappposelli and Davidson publicly embarrassed and humiliated McKeever by reducing his salary considerably for no substantial reason. For political reasons they had no problem taking away this man's ability to support a family of five children all in the name of political retribution. In 2001, Mayor Randee Davidson fired McKeever and replaced him with a truck driver to head a department that, in my opinion, required more leadership ability and competency than Kenny Petrone could muster. That observation of Petrone is based on his performance evaluation as an employee throughout his tenure. The increase in salary for Petrone by Council was proof positive that politics can pay if you know the right people and Petrone was indeed the right puppet for this regime. Davidson's political shenanigans repaid a personal political debt. However, for the people, the quality of Municipal Services went into a slump.)

(On the subject of Joe Esposito, I would be remiss in not disclosing a few details. In the election of 2000, Esposito ran against me in the Republican Primary along with former Councilperson Ginny Weber. I defeated both soundly. These two so-called Republicans then publicly supported Davidson in the November general election. Upon taking office, Davidson appointed Esposito to the Zoning Board of Adjustment as his reward. Esposito was always in need of the public's attention and in my 12 years as Mayor his lobbying for an appointment fell on deaf ears. I had a reason for denying Esposito an appointment because, in my opinion, he demonstrated an obstreperous attitude. He was a man so craving for personal recognition and personal financial gain that it was quite apparent that he would do little to enhance the philosophy of my administration's motto: "The People and the Township first and foremost.")

Visiting School Children is Fun!

A day with Dr. Suess. Where is the Mayor's hat?

It seems as though the children are enjoying the story as much as the Mayor.

What could be better? Reading stories to Elementary School Children, an annual event in New Jersey.

Education is My Number One Priority

Assemblyman Luongo pays a visit to the College of New Jersey and visits with several students enrolled in the Governor's School for the Arts.

Assemblyman/Mayor Luongo addressing the New Jersey Conference of Mayors on the topic of Violence in our Schools.

Assemblyman Luongo making a presentation on Scholarship funding for New Jersey's high school graduates with an overall 3.5 GPA. The HOPE Scholarship Program.

Legislators Working Together

South Jersey's finest Legislative team, working for all the people. Assemblymen Luongo, Geist and Senator Matheussen.
This legislative "Dream Team" conducted extensive town meetings in their district
and returned millions of dollars in State-aid to their constituents.

Politics is the art of compromise. "We can solve this problem."
Assemblymen Luongo and DeCroce working together!

Assemblyman Luongo leads a focus group of New Jersey's mayors dealing with the topic of taxes and municipal budgets.

Assemblyman Luongo conducts a press conference at the NJCM Convention in Atlantic City, NJ on the subject of Violence in New Jersey's Schools.

A Community is All About Family

Municipal monuments remind us that we will never forget those men and women who have served in defending our nation.

Hopefully we will leave those that follow us a better place in which to live.
Time Capsule 2020 opening!

One of many young families who moved to the Township because of the superior schools and public services.

"All elected officials need to make time just to sit and talk with the residents."

A strong religious presence in the community demonstrates the presence and importance of strong family values.

"To me, family is so important. Spending time with them can only make me a better person."
Mayor Luongo with grandsons Dillon (held) and Matthew, Jr. looking on.

Memories of People, Places and Events

Welcome to
Washington Township
South Jersey's
Premier Community

Dr. Gerald J. Luongo, Mayor

Assemblymen Luongo and Geist posing for a photo-op with
"Little Miss USA."

"It is important to recognize Veterans and their contributions to Keeping America Free." Gerald J. Luongo, Mayor

Assemblyman/Mayor Luongo addresses a group of Veterans on the issue of health benefits.

Chapter 17

DO WE REALLY NEED ELECTRICITY?

Most of us take for granted that the utilities that are part of our daily living will always be there. Except for the inconvenience of having our service interrupted, not much thought is given to public utilities other than perhaps paying the monthly bill. As more wonderful people decide to move into a community the demand for certain public utilities is requested and is increased exponentially. The company responsible for these public utilities, by law and under State statutes, must provide the service as demanded which is created by customer's use. Furthermore, any expansion of facilities, rate changes or other relevant factors affecting customer service must be approved by a Board of Public Utilities. Meetings of this Board are advertised and the public is invited and encouraged to attend and to give testimony. The control that local government has over a public utility—unless that government is providing said service—is non-existent. Once a public utility receives approvals from a Board of Public Utility, they will do what it takes to provide continuous and uninterrupted service to their customers.

The bulk of information relative to Atlantic Electric's (Conectiv) expansion plans were misunderstood by the self-appointed community advocates who opposed the plan. As I reflect on that time in my administration, I have come to the conclusion that these community advocates, although well intentioned for the most part, were disseminating partial and inconclusive information that supported their opposing view, but often lacked the facts that would prove their conclusions to be defective. Given the fuel needed to ignite the controversy, thanks to a Zoning Board member and two Council persons, what should have been a civilized understanding of a need created by the people turned into a controversy that pitted neighborhoods against one another. Residents became involved in scientific areas of research of which they had neither the expertise nor the understanding. Melodramatic public outbursts by individuals who tried to place fear in the minds of many residents ignorant of the facts became all too common. The weeks of public badgering at meetings, and the diatribes of uninformed Council persons who were clueless on the subject, dragged on much too long with absolutely no useful, productive or altruistic purpose. They began to cloud the issue and the salient facts. Additionally, such a protracted argument resulted in the people losing ground and the Township spending too many of the taxpayers' dollars to prove what the administration already knew to be true. Attempts to present the informed position on the subject at public meetings were met with jeers. To the many residents who tried to resolve this conflict in earnest and by working in a positive, collegial fashion, you are to be congratulated. For those residents who permitted themselves to be made pawns of the politicians and their cronies in order to attack the administration, welcome to the ugly side of local politics. And finally, to that handful of mercurial individuals who refused to accept the incontrovertible facts, what were you thinking? Maybe I should ask those individuals, "Who gave you the right to frighten, deceive and mislead so many good people in this community?" I do believe that to be a rhetorical question since many people know who you are, know your mentors and know the motives behind what you tried to do but rightfully failed.

In the early part of the 1990's, Atlantic Electric had received the approval of the New Jersey Board of Public Utilities to construct a non-generating substation. This was a distribution station to serve the electrical demands of the Township's growing needs. For those of us who had moved to the Township in the 1960's, we were all too familiar with blackouts and brownouts. Any minor rain or snow storm could interrupt electrical service for hours. The problem was exacerbated in the 1970's when the natural gas shortage forced builders to install electric heat pumps, electric hot water systems and all electrical appliances. As homes continued to be constructed in the 1980's, very little was done to improve electric service. Given the larger homes being constructed and the upswing in commercial development needed to offset the prospect of higher property taxes, the electric utility was obligated to improve service to ensure that the demands of its customers were met without exception.

As stated previously, the New Jersey Board of Public Utilities is the governmental agency to whom utilities answer and who determines rates, expansions and mergers. The local government has no authority in these matters. Atlantic Electric had an option to purchase a small farm located at the intersection of Greentree Road and Pitman Downer Roads adjacent to the Birches West Housing development. The site was near the source of 64k lines and would permit easy-in/easy-out for the transmission and distribution lines on pre-existing poles. The family had owned the farm site for years and quietly accepted the developing of Birches West on their property line, taking away their view as well as impacting their property with noise, run-off water and kids playing on their property. People in the neighborhood had forgotten that this friendly, unimposing couple had their retirement nest egg invested in that property, which they could sell for $1,000,000. These folks had resisted the temptation to sell their land on several previous occasions to housing developers when in fact houses were being built around them. The 12 acres was selling for $85,000 per acre and continues to be the highest price ever offered for an acre of farmland in the Township. As required by the Board of Public Utilities, Atlantic Electric was required to have a public hearing. It was scheduled at one of the local schools and properly advertised in all the area newspapers. This process takes place throughout New Jersey and in other communities in other states. The electric company and the property owners were in for a rude awakening.

Between the announcement of the meeting and the scheduled date, certain individuals began passing out fliers that implied that the site would be a generating station causing a negative impact to the residents, referencing electromagnetic fields (EMF) that were *alleged* to be a cancer-causing agent in children. Some fliers stated that I had given approval for the site based on either a financial interest or closeness with the property owner. Both assertions were outright lies! Of course, the fliers had no name taking responsibility for the information but whoever did publish it made sure that my office phone and home phone was prominent. (My home phone has always been in the book, but including it on the flier intimated that it was unlisted.) The number of calls proved that the flier, albeit inaccurate and misleading, was nevertheless effective.

The school auditorium was packed to standing room only. Residents, local, county and state elected officials, Board of Education members and of course the press were all present and accounted for without exception. The electric company officials were responsible for conducting the meeting and to explain what would be done and to answer all questions. They were prepared with all their information in a professional manner and attempted to conduct an informational and educational forum in hopes of establishing a dialogue with the residents. Although I had lived in the Township since 1969 and had experienced some very ugly and unpleasant meetings, especially as a nine-year member of the Board of

Education, you somehow hold out hope that meetings such as this will not erupt into ugly, uncivilized demonstrations of people at their worst. But many residents began to speak abusively and incite chaos. They refused to listen. The thought of yet another negative headline in the press generated by the unthinking and shortsighted public denigrating one of South Jersey's outstanding communities.

The owners of the farm sat there, totally unprepared for such attacks that at times, questioned their integrity and purpose in "hurting the residents." I can only imagine their feelings of humiliation and despair. Even with all the documented and empirical information provided by the electric company, the company's professionals continued to respond to questions from the public on information gleaned from what the residents had heard in the neighborhood, what they read in *Reader's Digest*, the supermarket tabloids or what was told them by family members who were allegedly informed on the topic of EMF's. Adding to this confusion, we had the posturing politicians, the disparaging remarks shouted out from the crowd and the inability for the crowd to be sufficiently silent in order to hear responses. Regrettably, nothing was accomplished.

Finally out of sheer frustration and the desire to get the hell out of that meeting, the property owner stood and addressed the crowd in a quiet, almost apologetic, voice saying simply, "My wife and I have decided not to sell our property." The crowd burst into applause as the property owners walked quietly from the room. The high-fives, the shouts of victory and the self-serving congratulatory statements to the crowd's leaders were to be very short lived. After the noise began to die down, the spokesperson for Atlantic Electric announced quietly that they would seek out another site and, regardless of what the people wanted, the sub-station would be built in Washington Township and that was a promise! An uneasy, almost eerie, silence fell over the crowd, stopping the self-styled luminaries and politicians from mugging for the cameras and hoping that a reporter might include their remarks in tomorrow's story. The crowd suddenly realized that this meeting was not the end, but rather the beginning of what would become an expensive, protracted and life-learning experience in the art of compromise and negotiations with big business.

Atlantic Electric had everyone's attention as it explained its position. The need to provide electric service at peak daily demands as well as the amount of electricity being used by the residents and the importance of the electric company's ability to transfer power to other lines in order to keep the power flowing, even during heavy weather and/or accident. The electric company, to its credit, gave testimony supported by studies of leading scientists, doctors and engineers relative to EMF and its effect on the body. These were studies based upon empirical research, not on feelings, emotions or hysteria. All this information and data was appropriately displayed in charts, graphs and published studies readily available to the public.

At this point many residents from the Birches West, who no longer felt threatened due to the fact that the property in question was no longer in the picture, left the meeting. Those residents remaining addressed possible solutions to the dilemma, including conservation by reducing electrical use or eliminating electrical appliances, converting to gas or oil and whatever—all to no avail. Township residents already had a difficult time conserving water as part of an entire region's effort to reduce water usage. The electric company and many of the residents were intelligent enough to realize that such a conservation plan was wishful thinking and would never work! At this point one resident stood and asked, "What are our alternatives?" The response to that question by the Atlantic Electric spokesperson would thrust me into the center ring, a position that was deleterious for any Mayor.

The spokesperson for Atlantic Electric recommended that the Township form a Blue Ribbon Committee to determine the best location for the sub-station in the community. The Blue Ribbon Committee (BRC) would explore the concerns of the residents, examine the parcels of available ground, speak to the property owners and reach out to professionals selected by the BRC to meet with the professional staff of Atlantic Electric. If the costs associated with the relocation of the proposed substation were within the proposed budget of Atlantic Electric's plan, the Blue Ribbon Committee's recommendation would be accepted and the project would move forward. Of course, the Blue Ribbon Committee would be chaired by the Mayor. The crowd agreed! I knew immediately that I had been drawn into a situation that was untenable. Regardless of the BRC's decision, some neighborhood in the Township would be unhappy with that decision and that I would be the scapegoat for this. But philosophically speaking, there are upsides and downsides to being Mayor. Local elected officials are held more accountable by the people than any other elected position, excepting perhaps Governor or President. The accessibility factor places the Mayor at the top of the list!

With ads placed in the local and area newspapers and direct mailers sent from the Mayor's Office to every resident, sufficient contact had been made explaining the purpose of the Blue Ribbon Committee, its goals and objectives, thus due diligence had been met. Anyone wishing to be a member of the committee simply needed to come to an initial meeting that would provide a forum for questions and answers. From that point forward, meetings were scheduled on a bi-monthly basis at the high school. After the initial two meetings, the number of volunteers settled at about 25 concerned residents. Contrary to political rhetoric, the Blue Ribbon Committee was not handpicked by the Mayor. Membership was open to anyone who really cared to get involved!

In addition to the volunteers on the committee, I provided members of the Township's engineering firm, two Planning Board members and the Township's Planner. (The engineering firm and the planner had to be paid at their hourly rate, a cost that was absorbed by the Township's budget.) The electric company provided a spokesperson, an engineer and scientist. Without getting into the minutia of the BRC's scope of investigation, suffice to say that the following areas of concern were addressed in painstaking detail:

1. The location of the substation in relationship to residential areas in terms of distance that the BRC agreed must exceed the State's mandated regulation.

2. The type of transmission poles and their locations to exceed State requirements.

3. The substation must be located adjacent to commercial or industrially zoned property.

4. The entrances and exits to the site must be on to state or county roads.

5. The entire substation must be fenced.

6. All service and supply lines must follow county or state roads with no crossing of farms, residential property, schools, churches, hospitals, or recreational sites in the planned routing.

7. Periodic testing would be done to determine the degree of EMF's being emitted from the transmission lines at the base of the poles.

Atlantic Electric agreed to all the parameters established by the Blue Ribbon Committee and this information was released to the press and included in the Mayor's newsletter requesting input from the public. The response was limited and the one concern was whether or not the lines could be buried to avoid the poles and the exposed wires. This was discussed by the Committee and a request made to the electric company. Due to the fact that the lines must be buried in conduit filled with oil to absorb the heat, it was determined that the process was too expensive and unnecessary and that servicing this kind of installation was a protracted process. The parameters established by the Blue Ribbon Committee restricted the number of sites that would be acceptable.

After a period of about seven months, the BRC had answered every question posed by the public. At the conclusion of this process of investigation, the electric company announced that it had an option on purchasing a parcel of property that met every requirement established by the Blue Ribbon Committee on behalf of the people. The parcel was located at the intersection of Fries Mill Road and Hurffville-Cross Keys Road to the rear of the Riggins Service Station, adjacent to property zoned industrial and with access to only county roads. The work of the BRC was completed and I thought the matter to be closed. Once again, I didn't see the storm clouds that were forming.

Two weeks had passed since the announcement of the sub-station was made in the press. There was no response from the public, so I assumed that the public understood what needed to be done. I have been taught never to assume anything and believe me that was a lesson well learned. There was a call from a resident by the name of Mrs. Renae Meehan. As always, I took the call. Mrs. Meehan indicated that she represented a group of residents from Scotland Run and Twin Ponds East, two developments that were closest to the site of the proposed substation. I found it incredible that anyone in Washington Township could be ignorant of the Citizen's Blue

Ribbon Committee, given all the press. Sensing Mrs. Meehan's fragile emotional state on the subject, especially her constant referencing of EMF and cancer in children, it would be pointless to rehash the events leading up to the announcement. I therefore invited her and any members of the committee that she represented to my office for a meeting. Shortly thereafter, Mrs. Meehan and her friend Mrs. Carol Schwartz of Twin Ponds came to my office. Both ladies were weighted down with reports, articles, a petition signed by homeowners and a video tape that supported their assertion that EMF's were a cancer-causing agent. I explained to them the process utilized in reaching the decision as to the substation's location. Their rebuttal was focused on whether or not Scotland Run and Twin Ponds residents were "invited" to join the committee. I explained the process utilized in composing the membership of the BRC. They retorted that two Councilpersons and a Zoning Board member told them that the committee was selected by me to ensure the selection of the site because "friends of mine would benefit"! I thought to myself, "Here we go again! The politicians are preying on well-intentioned individuals to do their dastardly deeds." Realizing that arguing with the uninformed who are steadfast in their position is sheer folly, I agreed to attend a meeting of the residents at Mrs. Meehan's home.

I came to the meeting and distributed a packet of information that dispelled all the misinformation that this group of residents had accumulated and which unequivocally supported the position of the Blue Ribbon Committee. It also described the process utilized in arriving at that decision by the BRC, plus a certified copy of the land's ownership. Unquestionably my presentation repudiated the lies of the two unnamed Councilpersons and the Zoning official. (I later discovered the identification of the three officials to be Councilpersons Bob Berry, Ginny Weber and Zoning Board member Bruce LaMonica. They were Republicans, as were Mrs. Meehan and Mrs. Schwartz. At that time, I was a Democrat. To the best of my knowledge, I did not let this political overtone affect my addressing of their concerns.)

Although the residents present at the meeting had studies and a substantial number of articles defending their position, it was countered by the more up-to-date, reliable and empirical scientific studies that I presented. A few residents were educationally qualified to discuss the issues objectively, but their position nevertheless, paled when compared to that of leading scientists throughout the world, whose studies on the effects of EMF had been published in leading medical journals. As well intentioned as the residents may have been, the bottom line was that they believed their neighborhoods the victims of political expediency, a theme that would be replayed by other neighborhoods as the Township continued to grow.

I thought over the results of this neighborhood meeting and their positions which seemed adamant. I concluded that I had three possible alternatives:

1. Reject the argument of the residents on the sound basis that everything was done properly and the decision of Blue Ribbon Committee was final.

2. Disregard the decision of the volunteers who served the Blue Ribbon Committee, ignoring all their hard work, and go back to square one.

3. Solicit from these residents not pleased by the decision their solution to the matter given its present status.

I was sufficiently *au courant* to realize that if I acted upon alternative number 1, the politics of all this would become a regular debate at Council meetings, providing our elected officials the opportunity to pander, stroke, cajole and play the political game for the residents, attempting to blame the Mayor for what would be reported by the press as a debacle. I decided to select alternative number three since I believed that this approach to be fair, honest and above all, it would leave the door open sufficiently to provide for compromise. The residents subsequently met a few more times before I was invited back to their meeting, at which time they made the following requests:

1. To have members of their committee meet with the Board of Public Utilities in Trenton, New Jersey.

2. To have access to all the information on the sites investigated by the Blue Ribbon Committee.

3. To select a scientist to review all the information available to date and to hold a public forum to solicit public input and to render a decision on his findings at a public meeting opened to all interested residents.

I accepted their three requests without any changes or deliberation. With the help of my good friend, former Senator John Mathuessen, we were able to arrange a meeting with the Board of Public Utilities, at which time representatives from the residents' group spoke openly and without any time constraints. I contacted the scientist that they requested and made all the arrangements for his visits to Washington Township. They had chosen Dr. Bruce R. McLeod, Professor of Electrical Engineering, Montana State University at Bozeman, who was an eminent scientist and whose published studies on electro-magnetic fields were recognized internationally.

Dr. McLeod made three visits to our community. The first visit enabled him to review all the materials that were used in the decision-making process. Dr. McLeod was taken on a tour of all the sites and was provided a complete set of demographic and aerial maps (three days). The second visit included town meetings with interested citizens and/or neighborhood groups to solicit questions and concerns (two days). The third visit was to meet, discuss and examine all plans and to establish a dialogue with the team from Atlantic Electric that included engineers, scientists and medical authorities and a representative from the Board of Regulatory Commissioners (six days). (These meetings spanned a time period of approximately three months.)

The final report of Dr. McLeod would be presented at a special public meeting announced one month in advance with one bi-monthly reminder distributed to all residents via messenger to ensure an interested audience. I informed Dr. McLeod that I did not want advance knowledge of the report and that I wanted to hear it for the first time along with the residents. The same school building where this entire situation unfolded almost a year before was selected as the meeting place. To the credit of the resident volunteers who served on the Blue Ribbon Committee, they sat in the front row. Considering how they were insulted and maligned by other residents unhappy with their decision, their presence spoke volumes as to their character and integrity. Notices were also sent to all official boards of the Township and of course Council. Along with Atlantic Electric and the press, everyone was present and accounted for without exception.

Dr. McLeod reviewed all the meetings that he attended and discussed the various concerns shared with him. He spoke to his on-site inspections of all the available sites and he discussed in detail, Atlantic Electric's plan with handouts, charts and graphs. He also provided a lengthy resume of his career, plus selected articles that he had written and articles written by other authorities on the subject of EMF, some who agreed with his position and others with opposing positions. Dr. McLeod provided a bibliography and encouraged residents to read substantial books and articles on the subject of electro-magnetic fields and not simply get their information from TV talk shows, supermarket tabloids or condensed reading such as *Reader's Digest*. He told the people that they were making an emotional debate of a subject that should be review scientifically and medically. After all this, the scientist selected by the residents' committee headed by Renae Meehan and Carole Schwartz, announced that the plan submitted by Atlantic Electric was without flaw and exceeded the normal requirements of the industry in order to ensure the health and safety of all residents. He concluded that the final report of the Blue Ribbon Committee was "outstanding" and that the site chosen for the substation was excellent. His printed report was made available to everyone and included the details of his verbal presentation and ultimate conclusions. His work was done!

I anticipated that if the report did not support the residents' predetermined decision, they would be unhappy. Dr. McLeod began to experience a barrage of negative statements and attacks on his credibility and integrity. As a professional selected by the residents and as a man who had the required expertise to make such a decision, he simply closed his notebook and quietly left the room. Regardless of those who could not accept the truth, this meeting was over. The only thing that remained to be done was to pay the bill generated by this entire protracted process, which many thought unnecessary since it yielded the same results as the volunteer Blue Ribbon Committee did for free. The presence of the substation today is a reminder that the matter was successfully brought to closure. To date, there has not been one confirmed reported case of illness that can be linked to electromagnetic fields in the area of the substation. In order to address the concerns of those few citizens, the Township taxpayers spent $250,000.

Chapter 18

WATER, SEWER, THE MUA AND MORE

Perhaps one of the most controversial appointed boards that I have ever had to deal with was the Municipal Utilities Authority. As with all authorities formed under New Jersey State Statutes, the MUA had a broad-base autonomy from its appointing authority, the Township Council. Under the form of government selected in 1985, Council was provided with the sole appointing authority to the MUA, Zoning Board, auditor and Township Clerk. As with most New Jersey authorities, they apparently answer to no one, especially not to the people. Board members either receive compensation in the form of direct salaries and/or exceptional health benefits packages and other perks that may include an automobile, credit cards, travel, conventions and much more. The Executive Director is a political appointment, overpaid and usually the person not the most competent or qualified for the job. I believe this to be the case relative to the Township's MUA.

Over the years the MUA was the focal point of numerous newspaper stories and outcries from the community about its exceptionally strong financial picture, escalating rates, failure to expand services in the best interest of the community, lucrative professional appointments and a condescending, arrogant and cavalier attitude that was indifferent, insensitive and to put it bluntly, rude! In my 12 years as Mayor, not once did I see the MUA initiate a creative plan to provide water and sanitary sewer to areas of the community where a developer did not pay for the infrastructure. Since the MUA controlled the issue of forms/permits that determined whether there was an adequate supply of water and sufficient capacity for sewer treatment, the latter was controlled by yet another politically based County authority, the Gloucester County Utilities Authority, appointed by the County Freeholders. Developers were basically held hostage and would agree to practically any improvement in order to get their project before the Planning or Zoning Boards. More than one developer lamented the manner in which both authorities conducted business and the pandering that went on from authority members in soliciting political contributions for local, county and state politicians and their respective political parties. For the seasoned developer, the realization that there was a cost for doing business in Gloucester County came as no surprise. These "hidden" costs were simply passed on to the buyers or leaseholders of their respective properties.

This method of developing an infrastructure for water and sanitary sewer is extremely lucrative to an authority. Once the infrastructure is completed, having been constructed to the authority's specifications, the developer deeds the system to the authority, who in turn charges the unit owner a tie-in fee and assesses monthly or quarterly charges for the water and sewer services. The MUA and the GCUA oversees the maintenance of the infrastructure, but that cost pales in comparison to the developer's up-front costs. For the MUA, it's a win-win situation and one that enriches their respective coffers. Once you get beyond the political rhetoric of the board members who are always crying "poor mouth," you can fully understand the ultimate power that this authority has over the developers, the residential community and commercial subscribers. Compound this power with an independent arrogance so vividly demonstrated by the chairperson and then imitated by other authority members, the Executive Director and many of the employees, you have what is called a dynasty!

I am not going to spend a lot of time focusing on the shortcomings of the MUA's leadership. Suffice to say that its chairperson for many years, Val Orsimarsi, was able to avoid the political minefields and remain in power through both Republican and Democratic administrations. The Czar remained the boss, controlling everything about the direction that the MUA would take. The members of that Board, no matter who they were, followed the Czar regardless of their personal opinion, if indeed they had one. When the MUA had the opportunity to appoint a new Executive Director it didn't look beyond the old boy's network. The MUA Board chose not to look for an Executive Director that would bring new, fresh, creative and innovative ideas as to the operations of a public service that really needed to be subscriber friendly and not simply a political cash cow. Rather the Czar appointed Shelly Belson, an old familiar political figure from the 1970's, who would surely follow the party line and the dictates of Czar Orsimarsi. There would be nothing new under the Belson umbrella of leadership, just more of the same old rhetoric. The appointment of Belson would prove to cause the Board a lot of grief in the future, ultimately leading to the downfall of Czar Orsimarsi. And in the final analysis, I do believe that Orsimarsi turned his back on me in my attempt for a fourth term as Mayor. He knew that when I was approached by my friend Councilman John Szczerbinski, asking that I make a deal with Councilpersons Lyons, Rappposelli and Davidson that would guarantee his reappointment to another five-year term, I said no. I would never make a deal with any of those three politicians, whose integrity and honesty was then and will always be a point of concern. And frankly, I didn't owe Orsimarsi or Shelly Belson one single thing!

This same type of political control manifested its ugly face at the Gloucester County Utilities Authority under the iron fist of Steve Sweeney and the various Gloucester County Democratic Committee Chairpersons. Like so many authorities, money and jobs were abundant and public accountability minimal. The GCUA probably had some of the shortest meetings on record. Many of the rank-and-file party loyalists would beg to be appointed to this board. "Boss" Sweeney was feared and everyone knew that if you went against what he wanted, your days in politics were numbered. Too many Democrats and Republicans who were the victims of this tyrannical individual and who experienced his blustering exhortations and haranguing knew what it was like to be in Sweeney's line of fire. It was Sweeney's way or no way and the Boss simply did not condone disloyalty, real or perceived.

In my 12 years as Mayor, I recollect that three major issues involving the MUA came to shake my confidence in their operation and their uncanny *inability* to think outside the box. Excluded from this criticism is the staff who worked in the engineering division and the workers who served the public 24/7 in dispensing their duties in a professional, courteous and efficient fashion.

RATE INCREASES

I understand fully the process that the MUA must follow in seeking approval for rate increases, which included petitioning the Board of Regulatory Commissioners. In the early summer of 1994, residents began calling the Mayor's Office complaining of excessive charges for water. Considering that the Township was part of a statewide water-conservation program, the residents were perplexed as to why their bills were so high. According to the residents, calls to the MUA were not returned, or in many instances the response from the MUA staff was simply that the resident was using too much water and needed to cut back. However considering the brown lawns, dying vegetation and the lack of blooms in season, it was obvious that many residents were depending on Mother Nature, who was not cooperating. To add insult to injury, many residents who could not afford to pay their MUA bill were served with shut-off notices. Since the MUA had assumed an indifferent attitude towards the residents, I was expected to do something to rectify this unfortunate turn of events, especially when residents were told by the MUA office staff, "If you don't like our answer, call the Mayor's Office" and so they did.

After much cajoling of Council (remember they appoint the MUA Board) they agreed to have representatives of the MUA available to answer questions at a public Council meeting. I realized that the Republican Council members felt uncomfortable by placing their appointees in harm's way and especially Val Orsimarsi. But then again it was only proper that Council listen directly to the people on this issue. The MUA, true to form, displayed a less than affable demeanor towards the residents and Council. Rather than dealing head on with the problem, the MUA began to discuss changes in the rate schedule based on volume usage. Although not abstract, by the use of charts, graphs and referencing the financial losses experienced by the MUA due to conservation, the presentation was perceived by the public as sidestepping the matter at hand. The meeting solved absolutely nothing. Bills were expected to be paid when rendered although extensions were provided and shut-offs would stop if subscribers agreed to a payment schedule. (This was a hardship for many residents and therefore I paid their water bills that summer in the amount of $1250.00 from my re-election campaign.)

GRENLOCH-GARDENDALE SANITARY SEWER

As a Mayor, you often propose projects that may help a few people but at the same time may benefit an entire community. Projects in the name of health and public safety fall into that category. The Grenloch-Gardendale sanitary sewer extension project was, in my opinion, a community health concern.

The communities of Gardendale and Grenloch have been part of Washington Township for a long time predating any other housing development. Grenloch is one of New Jersey's older communities. While developers were proliferating Washington Township with homes, condominiums and apartment complexes, the MUA was making unbelievable sums of money with permits, tie-in fees and subscriber services. It also had an elaborate sewer system designed and constructed by developers under the MUA's guidelines. In all these plans, it seemed that no one on the MUA or any elected official or appointed member of a Township quasi-judicial board ever suggested extending sanitary sewer service to Grenloch and Gardendale. I found that incredible! Here we were quickly approaching the 21st century and this Township had two developed residential pockets of the community on 75' x 100' building lots encompassing a square mile of the community, and the residents are discharging waste into septic systems, many of those systems in less than optimum working order, as shown by the several overflows and generally unpleasant odors following heavy rains. When I inquired why this was permitted to happen, the answer was an obvious one: there were no developers to construct the infrastructure and the MUA wasn't going to invest its money. What was I thinking? Isn't this precisely the kind of project that an MUA should be doing? Isn't this what is called reinvesting in the community? Isn't that why autonomous authorities are created?

I approached the MUA with my idea that this was a worthwhile project, but it received a very cool reception. My argument for this project, that it was "in the public health," was rebutted with, "These residents can't afford it." Reluctantly, the MUA agreed to have their engineer provide me with an estimate for Gardendale, Grenloch and parts of Woodbury-Turnersville Road. The cost was well over $4,000,000. I hasten to add that the number included only the lift station and the main trunk lines. Laterals from the street to the homes and grinder pumps for below-grade homes would all be extra and, of course, the tie-in fees for the MUA and the GCUA were all extra. The argument against such a project was the fact that all other homes with sanitary sewer had the cost of all these items, as required, included in the price of the home, paid for by the purchaser directly. I cannot dispute that argument. Rather I chose to address it by stating that the health of all residents takes precedence over dollars, especially if ground water could be in jeopardy of contamination. Given the close proximity of Grenloch Lake and the head waters for the Maurice River, this project was essential and it was incumbent upon me to find the solution.

Three plans were prepared, offering various scenarios and financial data supporting the possible alternatives. I prepared a booklet outlining my plans, including a cover letter and an invitation for the residents to attend a meeting to discuss the plans. In this fashion the residents would have the time to review all the information and perhaps discuss it with their neighbors. An informed public is essential to having a meaningful and productive discussion resulting in a positive outcome. I was impressed by the comments, questions and positive attitudes displayed by the residents. That night, Township Council learned a good lesson in civics!

I proposed the issuing of a general bond that would include the construction of the sanitary sewer system infrastructure in Gardendale and Grenloch, with the paving of all streets and the reconstruction of sidewalks as needed. Residents would be responsible for the laterals and had one year to tie in to the system and get off the septic system. Tie-in fees to the MUA and GCUA would be held at a lower rate that was in effect prior to a recent increase that both agencies approved. This tie-in fee could also be paid over a 60-month, interest-free period. And finally, my office made arrangements with local banks to provide loans for the cost of the laterals and the closing of the septic systems. All this took a bit of arm-twisting at the MUA and the GCUA under less than what I would call a cooperative spirit. Nevertheless the project was completed in a timely and professional fashion.

Although my adversaries accused me of "buying votes," I never won Grenloch in a general election as either a Democrat or as a Republican when running for Mayor or the Assembly. I know it may be a foreign thought to many politicians, but some of us do what is right for the community and to hell with the votes. That's what leadership is all about!

THE JOHNSON ROAD PROJECT

The Johnson Road project was yet another opportunity for the MUA to demonstrate its willingness to think outside the myopic box that characterized its thought process during the reign of Czar Orsimarsi. Regrettably as this scenario will point out, the MUA did not have a vision for the future. If the MUA had to invest in the Township for a project that was not its idea, it would be a very, very tough sell.

When I took office in 1989, I assessed the immediate needs of the community. I put forth a set of first-term goals and subsequently a set of 10-year long-range goals. There were no secrets from the public and I discussed all these plans, goals and objectives with the press and on several cable TV shows on which I appeared on a regular basis.

Johnson Road is the most heavily traveled Township-owned road. A major link between Route 42 and the Berlin-Cross Keys Road providing access to Winslow, Gloucester Township, Sicklerville and Camden County, some 10,000 vehicles traverse it daily. Given the growth patterns in all those areas, it was essential that a master plan be developed for this crucial artery.

In the early 1990's I brought together the mayors of Monroe Township (Jack Luby), Gloucester Township (Sandi Love) and Winslow Township (Al Brown). With the assistance of the Delaware Valley Planning Commission and the engineering departments of Gloucester and Camden Counties, the mayors agreed to aggressively lobby for the following projects based upon our vision as to the future development of our respective communities:

a) Camden County—Complete reconstruction of Berlin-Cross Keys Road from the County boundaries to Route 73 at the Berlin Circle. This would include turning lanes and traffic signals.

b) Gloucester County—Complete reconstruction of the Berlin Cross Keys Road from the County boundaries to Glassboro Cross Keys Road, including a by-pass through the proposed commercial property adjacent to CR555 and the proposed corporate park bordered by CR555, Route 42 and Hurffville Cross Keys Road and Fries Mill Road. This would include improvements to Route 42 by the State Department of transportation.

c) A proposal to the Atlantic City Expressway Authority for an interchange with on/off ramps at Berlin Cross Keys Road and the AC Expressway.

d) Washington Township—A plan to jointly request funds from the State Department of Transportation for a total reconstruction of Johnson Road from Stage Coach Road into Gloucester Township and ending at Berlin Cross Keys Road. Included in this would be traffic controls at both ends of Johnson Road with the ability to permit full access in both northerly and southerly directions at the Johnson Road and Route 42 intersection.

(All these improvements have been completed thanks to the hard, dedicated and committed work of four mayors who crossed political lines and town boundaries to work together for the people. We also developed a prudent plan for the investing of local, county and state tax dollars in projects benefiting two counties, four municipalities and hundreds of thousands of people.)

e) One of two projects that I thought essential to round out these four projects was the realignment of Johnson Road at the intersection of Stage Coach Road to create a four-way signal controlled intersection that would decisively slow vehicular speeds on Johnson Road. The cost was prohibitive, and attempts to purchase a home required in order to widen the intersection failed.

f) The other project was offered to the MUA. Given the successful lobbying that I did in Trenton for a grant to re-build Johnson Road, I was convinced that this would be the ideal time to install sanitary sewer and water lines from the termination point at Whitman Square, the length of Johnson Road to the Camden County line. This MUA project would service all homes along the upper portion of Johnson Road, Lillian Avenue, Stage Coach Road, all homes in the Jones Lake area and Mango Court. Since there was a large parcel of land already approved for residential growth at a site adjacent to the county line, the developer could have been charged for offsite improvements, thus lessening the cost of the project.

No question about it—it was a major and costly undertaking. Given the growth pattern and the potential of quality development in this area, the investment by the MUA at the time could be easily recouped by 2010. The fact that Johnson Road would be totally excavated for reconstruction provided the ideal time for a joint effort that would be so very cost effective. After several meetings and many proposed conceptional plans from the engineers, the MUA's answer was no. If I felt that such a plan would be beneficial to the community, then the MUA felt it should be part of the Township's budget. As I have said before, the MUA is the public utility authority, not the Township. They really needed to reinvest in the future of the town. They chose not to!

This is just another example of a lost opportunity for the MUA to be proactive. This is one more glaring and obvious reason to disband authorities and to place those services under the direction of the local governing body. Throughout New Jersey, people would benefit from such an organizational change. In New Jersey, however, authorities are so politically entrenched that neither the Governor nor the State Legislature has the temerity to take such a bold step in abolishing them. Once again, it politics before the people!

Chapter 19

PARKS, RECREATION, VOLUNTEERS

T he quality of life is one very critical component in determining the desirability of a community. People do not want to move to a community that is failing or whose leaders demonstrate an attitude of contempt that leads to failure. In other words, if you put down the community for which you were elected to serve, you have committed a disservice to the people. If elected to serve and you permit yourself to be persuaded by the naysayer in setting the town's agenda, you are committing an act of disloyalty. If politicians paused for a moment to think about their actions, they would see that acts of political grandstanding can undermine the very fiber of a town's image which, if tarnished sufficiently, will lead to decreasing property values and loss of commercial ratables, creating a downward spiral and plummeting the town into a financial and social crisis.

When I speak about Parks and Recreation, I am addressing a critical and essential component of what constitutes a Premier Community. There is more to living in a community than a comfortable residence, public services, shopping and professional services and educational facilities. The average American needs to take time to experienced "down time" in order to live a richer, fuller life. This can be accomplished simply by getting in contact with nature or by participating in a non-structured physical activity. The New Jersey Commission of Parks and Recreation would support my philosophy on personal recreation.

Not too many mayors have the opportunity to establish the standard for recreational and/or park facilities in their community. In 1989 I was given that opportunity, a challenge that I welcomed with enthusiasm. My goal, without even putting pen to paper, was to construct the finest facility in all of South Jersey, keeping in mind the needs of every age group in the community. It was essential to keep a balance between organized sports, related activities and non-structured activities for individuals in every age group. Now that's a challenge for any elected official!

An assessment of the recreational facilities was first, followed by an open-space inventory and then a comprehensive study of recreational trends nationwide. This was done through researching empirical studies and determining what the recreational experts were predicting. The most obvious component of Washington Township's recreational program was the commitment and dedication of the resident volunteers who gave of their time and talent in teaching, guiding and encouraging our children in the many-faceted programs provided by the Township. Like so many other communities, we could never afford to pay for the services which these volunteers provided. Not only did these volunteers coach our children, but they also worked on the fields, constructed facilities, raised money and developed programs for gifted and handicapped kids. Although these unsung heroes never had a motto, might I suggest one: "Providing a Recreational Opportunity for Every Child."

Throughout my terms as Mayor, I made it a point to recognize every volunteer and as many children as possible who participated in athletic as well as non-athletic programs. My weekly cable TV show filmed in my office provided a forum to introduce these volunteers to the public and to recognize the achievements of our children. I took great pride in the achievements of every resident. These people are the heart of the community!

No volunteer program is without problems. Once you establish a Parks and Recreation Commission or board, and also provide the format for the creation of the various sports advisory boards to administer the programs, there is the potential for conflict. That is human nature! However, I would say that when I was asked to mediate disputes (not the most agreeable situation to find oneself in), a resolution could be reached if all parties involved were reasonable. Conversely, if either of the parties held tenaciously to their position without even a compromise, someone would be unhappy with the outcome. But the program must go on, regardless of these small setbacks. All those involved must realize that we are serving the needs of the children and not placating the individual agendas of a few dissident individuals. I reiterate that Washington Township residents owe a great deal to these volunteers, the community shall always be in their debt for a job well done.

In my last two years as Mayor (1999-2000), I was chagrined at the behavior of Council President Lyons and his attempts to undermine the Parks and Recreation programs in this community. His blatant disrespect to the employees assigned to oversee the programs, as well as his demeaning the contributions of the volunteers and his attempts to sabotage any program or project that I presented before Council, was shamefully political. His clandestine meetings with certain politically motivated Board of Education members in attempting to reallocate approved Township funds to other projects was unethical and unprofessional, and it violated the Township's Administrative Code. Even when called on this by Councilman Szczerbinski at public meetings, Lyons at first would deny it, only to recant it and then attempt to lie about it. Even when the facts proved to the contrary, Lyons arrogantly held to his lies. To make matters worse, his allies—Councilpersons Rapposelli and Davidson—would find no fault with this behavior. One would lie and the others would swear to it. Such unethical behavior and arrogance was repugnant!

I must add that the projects including a soccer complex, improvements to the WTAA site, additional lighted fields in the park, the pedestrian tunnel and the construction of two field houses were approved by both the Parks and Recreation Commission and the Advisory Boards. I did my home-work! Unfortunately Democrat Councilpersons Lyons, Rapposelli and Davidson would do everything in their power to stop progress in the Township as they prepared to place Davidson on the ticket for Mayor in 2000. The late Jack Trimble had given the order to put politics before all else so that he could ensure his control of the Township once Davidson was elected to office.

For many years prior to my election as Mayor in 1989, part of a developer's responsibility was to provide the Township with open space and, in some cases, to construct play areas for the residents. Regrettably my open-space inventory disclosed that much of the open-space land was not acceptable for recreational use due to the location and the cost of development. As to the developer's constructed play areas, it was quite obvious that they provided bottom-of-the-line equipment that no longer met the State-mandated requirements for safety and the construction was shabby if not downright inferior. (Within a period of about eight years, every developer-constructed recreational site had been rebuilt and all equipment replaced or permanently removed.)

It was abundantly obvious to me that developers were incapable of providing the quality of play areas deemed appropriate by the people of Washington Township. As time passed, the poor quality and shoddy construction of developers' community clubs would also become an issue that I would need to face. It was therefore agreed by the Planning Board and adopted by Council in the late 1980's that developers would be required to contribute $1,000.00 for each residential unit constructed to the Recreational Trust Fund. This money would be placed in this special account for the exclusive use of developing recreational facilities. The deeding of suitable open space by developers was improved upon when the Planning Board accepted my recommendation requiring a Phase I and Phase II environmental study of the proposed open space. *The final two components of this aggressive recreational Master Plan were Council's validation by Ordinance of my recommendation limiting ONE HOUSE PER ACRE, on the aggregate, with all remaining land being deeded as open space to the Township and the assessing of no more than .02 cents on the tax rate in any given year for the purchase of vacant land to be placed in the Township's Open Space Inventory.*

With these limiting safeguards in place, the days of developers building four, five, six and more houses to the acre were over. The impact building of the 60's, 70's and 80's had come to an end—and not a second too soon. The result of all this legislation brought about an increase in the value of homes already constructed, the construction of larger homes paying their fair share of property taxes, less residential building, premium per-acre cost of land, and more open and natural greenlands preserved and unspoiled. We also saw fewer spurts in registrations of school-aged children, thus controlling the prospect of escalating property taxes.

Having accomplished all this early in my first two terms, with the cooperation of a Republican-controlled Council, it was time to embark upon an ambitious $5,000,000 plan that would become the hallmark of South Jersey's Premier Community, the Washington Lake Park.

WASHINGTON LAKE PARK

The Township was fortunate to have acquired a beautiful, pristine parcel of property bordered by Hurffville-Cross Keys Road, Greentree Road and Chapel Heights Road through a combination of an outright purchase and Green Acres Funds. The Washington Lake had already been developed and hosted thousands of visitors during the week and on weekends from Memorial Day through Labor Day enjoyed the manmade beach, the magnificent lake, locker rooms, restrooms, a picnic area, pavilion and more. Being a Green Acres acquisition, State law required the facility to be available to anyone and not just the residents of Washington Township. In the 12 years that I was Mayor, the yearly budget always included funds to maintain and improve this facility.

Contiguous to the Township Lake were two parcels of property totaling several hundred acres of beautiful farmland with several areas untouched and in their natural state. The parcels purchased in the early 1980's under a Green Acres Trust Grant was an environmental paradise, providing a home to deer, all types of birds and small animals. The area was to be a major park for the Township, but it seemed that no elected official was confident enough to come forth, propose a plan of development, tell the residents the price tag and deal with the fallout of perhaps a tax increase, which would provide what was absolutely and unequivocally needed in this community: Washington Lake Park!

I made the decision to move ahead on this project, knowing in my heart that Washington Lake Park would be the centerpiece, the focal point, the axis and the polestar of this community. The first step was to select a professional whose reputation and quality of work was superior. It was Richard Drewes of Schoor DePalma Engineering and I appointed him to design and oversee the construction of this park. As time would pass in the design and construction of this park and other recreational facilities in the community, it would come abundantly clear that I had indeed made the right choice in engineers. The second step was to form a Steering Committee comprised of James McKeever, Director of Municipal Services; Mrs. Adele Riff, Recreation Supervisor; the Parks and Recreation Commission and me. Third, a notice was placed in the area newspapers inviting interested citizens wishing to participate in the developing stages of a park project to attend meetings and share ideas. The public's input was especially critical in directing the Steering Committee's thinking to ensure that this park would be a park for everyone.

Drewes attended all our meetings so that he could hear firsthand the discussions. After several meetings, the Steering Committee was able to develop a comprehensive inventory of what the park should offer. This was called Phase I. Realizing that we could not include everything suggested for the park and due to financial constraints, we then proposed a Phase II and a Phase III construction program. Capitalizing on many months of design, meetings, redesigns, questions, answers and numerous financial concerns, a final version of the Washington Lake Park was beautifully rendered in colorful detail ready for presentation to the pubic and Council. Frankly, I was not prepared for what was to come!

The public's attendance at this meeting was excellent and the general tone of the public was that we needed this park. The presentation was made before Council, and seated at that time were Councilpersons John Rogale (R), Leonard Simmons (R) (deceased), Ginny Weber (R), Robert Berry (D) (deceased) and Sam Hart (D). Excepting Weber and Berry, Council was receptive to the reasoning that the park should be constructed in phases and that a major investment in Phase I was essential. Predicated on the Township's growth, the expanding recreational programs and the need to focus our resources in one major area of recreational development, I was confident that we would move expeditiously on this project. Weber and Berry always found fault with any project presented that might impact the tax rate or require bonding. They were of the mindset that we should piecemeal the construction process and only build what we could afford to pay for in any one budget year. Their thinking was myopically regressive. Taking their thought process to its ultimate end, one would build a home, a school, a hospital, room by room over a protracted number of years. Bonding would provide a timely completion of a project and the repayment of that bond would be the responsibility of present and future taxpayers, with a minimal impact on the tax rate in any one year. At times, getting elected officials to think progressively is tantamount to swimming against the tide!

A major consideration in the planning process of developing the park was its perceived negative impact on the residents of Amesbury Farm, the development adjacent to the park. The developer of Amesbury Farms assured the Township that an announcement would appear in all literature to potential homebuyers that a Township park would be constructed on their borders. Despite that, residents had legitimate concerns. Attempting to deal with individual homeowners or those identifying themselves as the official spokespersons of the residents was impossible. I met with the homeowners, suggesting that they form a homeowners' association and work with their leadership in addressing their concerns in a unified fashion. The residents found an excellent leader in Joe Devine, who brought the development together, providing a democratic process for prioritizing concerns and who, in tandem with my office, resolved all apprehension. (Mr. Devine also worked closely with the Township in developing and seeing to fruition the numerous improvements to the Kennedy Medical Center, the Outpatient Surgical Clinic and the quality Assisted Living Complex.)

Over the next year we added to and modified the park. The inclusion of a skateboard park, amid much criticism, proved to be an excellent project that provided our youth (and adults) a safe haven for an activity that has no place on the streets or parking lots with makeshift ramps and obstacles that could lead to serious injury. Those using the skateboard park followed the rules, which included protective skating gear. Many other communities throughout the region fashioned their own skateboard parks, including design, rules, regulations and policies after Washington Township's Premier Skateboard Park. Once again my administration took those giant steps required in doing what needed to be done for the public, disregarding the naysayer and short-sighted and uncreative individuals who simply never possess a vision for the future. No comment of the subject of the skateboard park would be complete without applauding the efforts of the teenagers who staged a sit-in the Mayor's outer-office requesting that their voices be heard about the need for a skateboard park. I listened, I learned and I acted. Those teens and their parents, spent many hours working with Jim McKeever and me, along with Richard Drewes, in developing this skateboard park. Take pride, it was worth the effort!

Improvements were made to the street hockey court, the addition of soccer and baseball fields, lighted and quality tennis courts, an environmental center, boardwalks through environmentally sensitive areas of the park to serve as nature trails, and a cadre of other augmentation that garnered Washington Lake Park top honors in the *Courier-Post's* "Best of South Jersey" and the recognition and top award from the New Jersey Parks and Recreation Commission at their annual convention in Atlantic City, New Jersey.

The amphitheatre was my administration's final contribution to the Washington Lake Park. This is a magnificent structure that provides for the arts which, in my opinion, are the soul of any community. Thousands of people from throughout the area have enjoyed the Concerts in the Park Series and numerous special programs that enrich the lives of everyone who takes advantage of this outstanding outdoor performing facility. Combined with the Township's Center for the Performing Arts it is accurate to say that Washington

Township provides a cultural climate that enforces its position as South Jersey's Premier Community.

The number of letters and calls that I received about the park while I was Mayor speaks volumes to the fact that my goal was successfully achieved. That by itself is sufficient validation of my efforts and the efforts of the community-minded individuals who walked the walk with me to see a dream come true.

On the negative side of all this positive accomplishment, I cannot ignore how ugly and ignorant Councilpersons Lyons, Rapposelli and Davidson, along with their cronies, behaved during this final construction phase of the park. Although they try to take credit for these projects, they choose to forget what they actually and maliciously said and did, which is part of the record as noted in tapes and press reports of the meetings. These three Councilpersons join the likes of Ginny Weber and Bob Berry in their negativity towards any project that was progressive, creative and innovative. These people could not bring themselves to work with me to provide the very best for the people. For some inexplicable reason, they all chose to travel the low road on the political highway.

Grenloch Lake Park

Prior to 1999, Council (excluding Bob Berry, Joseph Yost and Ginny Weber) saw the need for making improvements to existing recreational facilities and neighborhood parks. The improvements to and the revitalization of Grenloch Lake Park was one such major project funded in part by Green Acres Trust financing. (The hamlet of Grenloch is a quaint section of Washington Township that is one square mile in area, bordering historical Blackwood and Lakeland, New Jersey. In the late 19th and early 20th centuries, rail service to the area brought many visitors from the city to enjoy cottage living and recreational activities, among them swimming, boating and fishing in Grenloch Lake and an amusement park.)

Realizing the proud heritage that many of its residents held to, it was essential that Grenloch Lake Park be designed with the input and approval of the residents. Once again, with the able and capable assistance of James McKeever and Adele Riiff, we met with the residents on several occasions at the original Grenloch Fire Hall. The meetings were productive and the result was the construction of a low-impact park consisting of a playground, baseball field, nature trails, fishing piers, restrooms, boat launches and an All-Veterans Memorial. With the help of various community groups, the entire area of wooded land from Grenloch to Route 168 was cleaned up over a period of months. For years this woodland area was treated as a dump by irresponsible people.

Over the years the dump at the Lapari Landfill in Pine Hill had contaminated the ground waters that fed Grenloch Lake. The lake had also become an illegal dumping area. Although the lake supported fish and other marine life, the water was not suited for swimming even though the water quality had improved since the Lapari Landfill was closed. A major project planned for my fourth term in office was to dredge and regain Grenloch Lake, and construct a water park. That dream was never to be realized!

As part of Grenloch's revitalization program, the Township purchased from the Fire District the original Grenloch Fire House.

Although Council balked at the $165,000 price tag, the Township kept the building out of the hands of developers and also provided money for the Fire District's plans to construct a much-needed fire house on Fires Mill Road. After several months of extensive remodeling and bringing the building into code compliance, The Grenloch Community Center was opened. One group of dedicated individuals found a home when the American Legion/VFW was provided a permanent location for their meetings and activities at no cost.

In politics they often tell you, "No good deed goes unpunished," and I soon realized what the expression meant. Vandalism of the park became a weekly activity for some very sick and demented individuals. The desecration of the Veterans Memorial was especially heinous. Municipal Services made repairs on a daily basis and police and ranger patrols were stepped up in order to apprehend the cowards who committed their ugly deeds under cover of darkness. Additional security lighting was added under carefully designed plans instituted by Conectiv Electric and agreed upon by the people. Regrettably certain residents felt that I was not doing enough for Grenloch and they complained first to the press and then to the Township. At least two residents from Grenloch attended Council meetings regularly in 1999-2000, complaining that I had abandoned the community. As time passed, I realized that this was a carefully orchestrated political attack, one of many created by the late Jack Trimble, Randee

Davidson's handler. A classmate of Councilwoman Davidson was leading the charge with her rhetoric and dramatic emotional outbursts at meetings. Subsequently the cowardly vandals were apprehended and to no one's real surprise, it was an inside job.

SENIOR CENTER

The Senior Center was yet another project that I look to with pride. For too many years, the seniors of this community were relegated to a few hours a week in the overused, inadequate and deteriorating Community Activities Center. Given the increasing number of seniors in the Township who had contributed to this community, it was time to give them something back. Under the strong leadership of a community volunteer, Vincent Grosso, the Senior Citizens Advisory Committee met with me and urged that I find a permanent home for them. The Advisory Committee wanted to provide a daily schedule of activities as well as special events so seniors could meet in friendship. I too realized the importance of such a center and the need to enrich the lives of our senior population, so I set about finding the solution.

First, a Senior Center must be centrally located in an area that provided high visibility and accessibility to those seniors who drove and to those who used the Township's senior ride. The location must also be adjacent to an improved traffic-controlled intersection, shopping, banking, professional and emergency services. We also wanted to avoid a typical block building or a flat piece of land that offered no aesthetic accouterments.

The examination of the Township's land inventory failed to produce the perfect site. However, I remembered that while serving on the Board of Education in the very early 1970's, we purchased an approximately 11-acre piece of property on Greentree Road west of Egg Harbor Road adjacent to Heritage Valley. I knew the School Board would eventually need to build a third middle school and its location would need to be in the vicinity of Twin Ponds East. The Township owned 25 acres of land on Pitman-Downer Road near the Glassboro/Monroe Township border. I approached then Superintendent Dr. Robert Kern with the proposal for an even swap of land. He was amicable to the swap, but of course the Board of Education needed to approve the deal.

What seemed to me to be a rather simple and direct plan that would demonstrate a cooperative spirit between two entities of governance somehow became complicated by a few politically motivated Board of Education members and of course, the destructive duo of Councilpersons Berry and Weber. I sat in utter amazement as Board Member Eileen Abbott (D) came to Council meetings with her lame questions and stall tactics that reeked of jealousy. Of course, not to be outdone by the Board of Education naysayer, Berry, Weber and their cronies rounded out the gloom-and-doom team. True to form, rather than finding ways to make this plan happen, this group of pigheaded and cantankerous individuals found every reason to say NO.

The motives of these invidious individuals eventually became apparent, which led the other members of Council and the Board of Education to vote their approval. Considering that the construction of the facility would be funded by the sale of a liquor license, there would be no impact on the tax rate. Once the Senior Center was constructed, Tom Donahue took over the reins of leadership of the Senior Citizens Advisory Council. This man truly committed himself to ensuring that the Senior Citizens of Washington Township had one of the finest centers and programs in the County. In fact, Donahue's Senior Lunch Program surpassed the County's program in the quality of food served and its low cost. (This independence did not set well with the County and both Mr. Donahue and I knew that there would be a price extracted for our defiance of "Boss" Sweeney and the Freeholders.) Donahue and his loyal board members provided recreation, education, socialization and entertainment for all township Seniors. In the late 1990's the senior demands on the building required the construction of a beautiful addition. I was humbled to have the addition named in my honor and I deeply appreciated the seniors honoring me in this fashion. After the election of 2000, Donahue was gratuitously removed from the Senior Citizens Advisory Board by Mayor Davidson because he would not be her puppet. Subsequently the photo and dedication plaque in my honor surreptitiously disappeared and Davidson was "looking into it." Thanks to some very honest people, among them Tom Donahue and Mrs. Fran Capetola, the plaque and the photo magically reappeared. According to unnamed sources, its loss was because of Councilman Lyons' directive to Kenny Petrone, the politically appointed Director of Public Works, to remove it. Caught red-handed in several lies, neither one had the integrity to admit what they had done. (Fran Capetola, her husband Art and their family, Joe and Dina Devine, and Fred and Joni Casta, have been loyal supporters through both the good times and the bad and I respect their friendship.)

As I reflect on the community's efforts in the construction of the Creative Playground and the Cricket Fields at Valley Green, the County House Road Soccer Complex, the WTAA Complex, the T-Ball ballfields, the Midget Football fields, the Girls' Softball fields and so much more, I would be remiss in not saying "thank you" to the volunteers, as well as Councilpersons Agnes Gardiner, Sam Hart, Jane Huesser, John Rogale, Leonard Simmons, John Szczerbinski and Tom Torchia who, regardless of political affiliation, shared my vision for a better Washington Township. What these people accomplished will never be duplicated nor will their successes be fully appreciated. These true servants of the public trust kept their politics out of governing.

Chapter 20

ROADS, DRAINAGE, TRAFFIC AND DAMS

I wanted to touch upon the problems that these four areas can cause any mayor, in any town or city, in anywhere, USA. Too often the general public expects solutions in these areas when in fact none exists. Too often residents of suburbia perceive themselves as a separate entity and do not realize that the government's function is to serve the needs of all the people. In a democracy, the needs of the majority must, at times, take precedence over the individual. We all pay taxes, but paying property taxes is not a valid reason to assume special treatment relative to one's complaint. In my 12 years as Mayor, I can state unequivocally that every complaint and every project was addressed in a decisive, impartial and professional fashion. Although residents may believe to the contrary, they are wrong! In many cases problems and/or complaints were resolved to the best possible extent and unfortunately, for the government, not to the unreasonable expectations of the residents. And in these cases, frankly nothing could appease them! This kind of convoluted and misguided thinking by some residents was reinforced through the years by the irresponsible and totally baseless statements made publicly by Councilpersons who had no idea what to do, but they enjoyed creating a contentious atmosphere in the community. As many of you may well know, "a simple solution to a complex problem is the thinking of a fool." Heading the list of fools, in my opinion, are Ginny Weber, Bob Berry, Joseph Yost, Ray Rapposselli, Mathew Lyons and, of course, Randee Davidson. I find it incomprehensible that any relatively intelligent person could subscribe to such deprecatory remarks about Township problems, services or its employees. No elected official has that right! Such behavior is loathsome and malicious and speaks to that official's character deficiency.

ROADS

The Township's major responsibilities regarding roads are to those internal arteries located within the residential developments. All other roadways, excepting a few, are the responsibility of the County or the State of New Jersey. Upon taking office in 1989, I was committed to improving roadways predicated upon a long-range plan based on need and not on political expediency. Under my direction, the Township engineer prepared a Comprehensive Road Improvement Program. Every Township road was inspected, measured and photographed as to problem areas. Sample borings were taken to determine the quality of the materials used in the original construction and/or the last improvements to the roadway. Past files were studied to determine all the repairs that had been made over a prior 10-year period. Also inspected and rated were storm drain inlets, sewer-access elevations, curbs and driveway aprons. From this mountain of information, every roadway was given a rating which determined the urgency of repairs needed. This information was shared with the MUA to determine if any water or sanitary sewer work was projected so that a jointure could be agreed upon, thus reducing the overall cost and reducing any inconvenience to the residents. Periodic updates were conducted and on the average, five to 10 roadways were improved each year, depending on available funds and Council's approval of long-term bonding. Emergency repairs were executed on an as-needed basis and I aggressively sought State grants, which at times enabled us to increase the number of roadway improvements to 15 or more projects per year. The public support of this method of determining need was quite rewarding. From this study it became abundantly apparent that many developers during the period 1965-1985 failed to construct the roadways in their approved sub-divisions to Township standards. Maintenance bonds had expired and the taxpayers were left to foot the bill for repairs.

DRAINAGE

One the major complaints from residents during my tenure as Mayor had to do with drainage. Given the fact that the majority of subdivisions were at one time farm land, the necessity for developers to design creative drainage systems, moving runoff water to the street and to storm drains, or overland to culverts and eventually to retention or detention basis was quite a feat. In the 40-plus residential developments in the Township, there exist very few piping systems on private property to move water underground. The principal method employed to address water runoff was either across one property to another and so on, eventually leading to the streets, or to move runoff water between two properties over the sidewalk and into the street.

At Planning Board meetings, engineers could carefully explain the handling of storm water based on the proper site elevations and grading of the property. It seemed fairly reasonable at first blush, but in application, it was quite a different story! The problem with this design is that it does not nor is it designed to take into account improvements or redesigns made to the property by the homeowner. The installation of a fence, patio, room addition, pool or extensive landscaping can drastically affect the original water runoff design, impacting not only adjacent properties but a significant number of properties within the development. When this occurs, you can be assured that several residents will be severely impacted by flooding. In many of these acute situations, neighbors were at odds with one another and, at times, they took their grievances to court. As in most communities in New Jersey, water runoff and drainage on individual properties is the sole responsibility of the property owner, not the local government. It is assumed by local officials that all work that takes place on private property is done in a manner that in no way impacts neighboring properties. This is usually not the case and the results can be devastating.

In trying to avoid neighborhood disputes, I took on the responsibility of at least having an on-site inspection of distressed areas by the Township's engineer, if possible, during storm conditions. When the cause of the problem was obvious, the offending property owner was notified to make corrections. In situations when the problem was not obvious, the engineer investigated further. If the problem was the Township's responsibility, it was repaired in a timely fashion. Regrettably during this process, it became evident that many improvements by homeowners had no building permits and therefore were illegal. For these homeowners, costly changes resulted. On the positive side, the Township took on the awesome task of reconstructing numerous detention and retention ponds deeded to the Township that failed to operate properly due to poor construction by the developer, or due to lack of maintenance in prior years. Although a costly undertaking, the Township addressed these problems and the number of drainage and flooding dwindled to only a few that would require costly major reconstruction.

TRAFFIC

Traffic is like politics inasmuch as everyone has an opinion and, depending upon your vantage point, you can be considered right, left or moderate. To the business community, traffic is important if not essential. Traffic to business America and Washington Township means more shoppers, more spending, increased profits, and more revenue in taxes for the Township coffers to support public schools and Township services. Business America produces all this without placing one child in the public schools or requiring any of the services which municipal government offers. Business is a win-win source of income for the public. Everyone benefits! A strong business base in a community indicates a healthy growing community, which in turn increases property values and stabilizes the tax rate. People choosing a place to live do not move to dying communities. Most residents will be honest enough to admit that they move to a community based on the quality of education, availability of services and a premier address.

Those folks who try to say that you can have all of this without traffic are out of touch with the reality of the situation. Residents need to look at their own driveways and streets to see just how many vehicles are at each home address. They need to examine the student parking section at the high school. They need to take a look at the school district's bus yard. That's a start for determining why we have so much traffic! Residents need to be honest in admitting how many trips they take daily for various reasons without attempting to carpool or walk. How many students drive to school rather than take the school bus, which must be provided by law whether the seats are full or not? Residents need to understand the traffic patterns of a community in terms of major county roads, state highways and local streets and the number of people who drive each day and the number of families who are transporting children and adults to various locations, seven days a week. Active communities create traffic, and there is no way of stopping it unless people stop driving and that is not a realistic solution. People who want to stop traffic are those who are so impatient they don't wait their turn to enter a major road from a development roadway. They are the drivers who try to beat every amber light or who never stop and look before making a right turn on red. Or who pass on the right, tailgate and simply disrespect others because of their impatience. Unless you live in a gated, guarded or private community anyone wishing to use that public roadway in front of your home has the right to do so. When I think about the tax dollars appropriated for traffic studies predicated on the complaints of residents who made an issue out of traffic for disingenuous reasons, I could kick myself. No matter what was spent on these studies and regardless of the outcome, if it wasn't what the residents thought the outcome should be, you were wrong. This is an absolutely NO-WIN SITUATION! To make themselves even more disagreeable, these residents and their compatriots tend to go to the press and insist that the Mayor never tried and could not care less if one of their children got hurt or killed. To that I answer, Rubbish! And the complaint that police never patrolled the streets, to that I also answer, Rubbish! Police did their best in patrolling all streets in the Township, in addition to answering other urgent calls for help, assistance and accidents. So often when traffic patrols gave citations in a neighborhood, 90% of the traffic offenders were residents of that neighborhood. So much for the outsider theory! Too many people had too much time on their hands when traffic became the focus of all their attention. Perhaps those who complain all the time about traffic and who can never be satisfied with the solutions, are simply WRONG!

DAMS

When Washington Township was 23 square miles of mostly farmland, orchards and woodlands with a few homes, landowners built dams to create private lakes and sources of irrigation during dry spells. Dams were constructed of earth and wood and served their purpose. Of course, these dams predate the creation of a State Environmental Commission and a Dam Commission. That was a much simpler, less complicated way of life! As the farmer's plow gave way to the developer's bulldozers, concrete and blacktop replaced Mother Earth and the natural order of percolation of excess water yielded to retention ponds (holding water for long periods of time) and detention ponds (holding water for 48 hours or less) that proliferated in the landscape. In theory, it's a plausible way of handling excess water, as long as the ponds are properly constructed and maintained, which does not describe the vast majority of ponds in this community prior to 1989. Both the retention and detention ponds had a major impact on the manmade and natural lakes and the dams that were never replaced or improved upon to handle the amount of water now being diverted. In the early 1990's the Dam Commission stepped up enforcement and inspection of all dams, both public and private. All dams in the Township were private and owners were surprised to be served with notices requiring repairs to the dams. The costs for these repairs were staggering. Frankly, the dam owners were victims of a situation created by the developers and seemingly overlooked by the Township in the planning and approval process. Numerous meetings with dam owners and the Dam Commission eventually produced a positive outcome. With the intervention and assistance of former State Senator John Matheussen and former Assemblyman George Geist, the State and the Dam Commission were made to realize that improvements to private dams, whose integrity was compromised by development and an omission by the Township, could not and should not be a financial obligation of the owners. Rather, if routine inspections determined problems, the Township and the State of New Jersey would need to work cooperatively in solving these problems. Under my leadership, millions of dollars were spent in reconstructing failed detention and retention ponds over a 12-year period. In many instances, developers charged extra for building lots located on "lakefront property" when in reality these so called "lakes" were run-off drainage ponds. Many residents had boat docks constructed and even created beaches at the edge of these ponds. Talk about misleading advertising, these developers wrote the book. And anyone who knows these early residential developers of this community knows who I am talking about. Although one or two have hung around town and have attempted to re-invent themselves, there are sufficient people who will always remember who you are and what you did *to* and not *for* this town. (And one little reminder guys, water cannot and will not run up hill on its own.)

No discussion of dams would be complete without quickly addressing two costly interventions by my administration. One such intervention was quite gratifying and the other is a perfect example of "no good deed goes unpunished." Let me get the negative one out of the way first since this was a situation that was exacerbated by Council's diabolic triad of Lyons, Rapposelli and Davidson and two unreasonable residents of a specific neighborhood who simply had unrealistic and unreasonable expectations.

Twin Lakes Dam This area of the Township is located off of Fish Pond Road located near the Glassboro boundary. A quiet area of perhaps 30 homes, it has two lakes that are principally fed by several retention/detention ponds in the area and a few underground springs that, for the most part, have been choked by sediment discharged into the lakes from the retention/detention ponds. The upper lake and the lower lake are separated by an earthen, reinforced dam that also is the principal roadway into the secluded area. The upper lake is owned by the Township, and the lower lake is privately owned by the property owners whose homes border the lake. All this information is recorded in deeds filed with the Tax Assessor's office clearly defining ownership. The lower lake had an earthen dam that had, through time and use, become an unofficial roadway. All water discharged from the lower lake through the dam made its way downstream into neighboring Glassboro.

During the early summer of 1991, the Township was hit with a devastating rain storm. Flooding throughout the town was widespread. The upper dam at Twin Ponds Lake was breached and several homes were flooded. Without the volunteers who filled and piled sandbags to stop the cascading water, two homes in that area would have been lost. Following that near disaster, it was apparent that work must be done to ensure the integrity of the dam and the roadway and to provide a fail-safe mechanism to prevent any such reoccurrence of flooding. A dam-restoration project requires the services of a professional engineer, approved by the State and the Environmental Protection Agency and the State's Division of Wildlife. The cost for such a restoration is well into the half-million-dollar range! This would be an expense borne by the taxpayers.

After completion of the upper dam restoration project, the residents living on the privately owned lower lake began complaining that the water level of their lake had dropped significantly and that any marine life was being destroyed. Their lake had become a mud hole! The Township engineer made adjustments to the upper, Township-owned dam, permitting the maximum volume of water to spill over the dam to the lower lake. Still the lower lake did

not maintain an acceptable water level. The residents insisted that the problem was related to their
dam, which they believed was breached by the MUA
when sanitary sewer was installed to service the
Constanzo development of Spring Lake located on
the other side of Fish Pond Road. The MUA dismissed
the residents' complaint out of hand as nonsense
and refused to be involved. The Township engineer
speculated that some water could be lost to the sanitary sewer project. Furthermore he was confident
that the amount of water finding its way through
the earthen dam was insignificant. The homeowners'
dismissed the engineer's theory as nonsense. As
Mayor, I was in the midst of this controversy. Although I knew that the Township had no business
on private property, I nevertheless engaged the
homeowners in a dialogue to see if a solution could
be reached. I should have dismissed the
homeowners' complaint. This was a private lake and
not the responsibility of the taxpayer. If anyone was
responsible it was the MUA and Mr. Constanzo!

To ensure the total involvement of the residents, I
conducted on-site meetings with the Township engineer and Jim McKeever, Director of Municipal
Service. The residents insisted, predicated on the
input of one very knowledgeable resident, that a new
dam was needed, one constructed of steel sheeting,
pilings and backfill with stone and concrete. Also,
the MUA's sanitary sewer line needed to be back-

filled and the area compressed due to shoddy construction in the original installation. In the 1994-
95 Township budget, I appropriated the funds for
the construction of a new dam. Construction was
completed in a timely fashion. From the first time
that I entertained the homeowners' complaints until the completion of the project, the homeowners'
were regularly updated by correspondence, mailed
and/or hand delivered to their homes. To everyone's
dismay, the new dam did not solve the problem! The
water level in the lake could not be maintained. Although the residents had walked through this
project through every step of the way, the dam failed
and the idea was now all my fault! Rather than accept the unfair criticism and walk away from this, I
was determined to show the residents that indeed
the Township did everything right!

I then employed the professional services of a hydrologist, whose proposal included the scoping of
the MUA's sanitary sewer lines in the neighborhood
and the installation of monitoring pipes in the area
to see if any water was escaping into faults and traveling underground parallel to the improperly back-
filled sanitary sewer lines. The hydrologist's theory
was correct! Water flowed regularly along and around
the sanitary sewer lines and percolated in a wet-
lands area near the woods. The project to repair it
cost $175,000. In a letter to the residents I explained
all this and provided a copy of the report. The resi-

dents dismissed this professional report as non-sense. Having no other options, I closed the file on Twin Lakes! In late 1999 or 2000, Joseph Bowe, a retired Township police officer and member of the Republican Party (my party) who lived in the neighborhood, appeared before Council stating that I did nothing to resolve the problem of the Twin Lakes Dam and the residents' complaints. Bowe was not involved in the process that I previously discussed in detail. Well, of course, the diabolic triad of Lyons, Rapposelli and Davidson feigned shock at learning that the Mayor did nothing for the residents of Twin Ponds Lake. The drama was obviously staged for political reasons. Shame on Joe Bowe for letting himself be used! As I said previously, "No good deed goes unpunished." (In the ensuing year, Joe Bowe and Renae Meehan, both Republicans who joined the Davidson bandwagon in 2000, ran for the School Board with the support of the Township's Republican Club. They both lost.)

Jones Lake Dam This story will highlight the integrity of hardworking residents who desired to solve a problem outside the political arena. During yet another torrential rainfall in the mid-1990's, a headwall controlling the storm management system from the Valley Green Development gave way, cascading thousands of gallons of water over Johnson Road and overland to Jones Lake with such force as to blow out the Jones Lake Dam. Jones Lake was a small body of water that was fed by several springs that eventually flowed downstream into neighboring Camden County. (Inspection of the headwall the following day provided a clear indication that Mother Nature was assisted by a person and a sledge hammer, possibly the work of a disgruntled contractor whom I was leaning on to correct the malfunctioning Valley Green Storm Water Management System. Just my opinion, mind you!) The few homes that surrounded Jones Lake had lost boat docks and manmade beaches, which had provided a lovely setting, increasing property values. The residents, led by a real gentleman, Richard Fackler, came to see me and asked if I could help. The residents would gladly share in the costs and provide whatever labor they could in reconstructing a dam. In contacting the State, I was informed that as long as the plans were sealed by a professional engineer and approved, who did the construction was immaterial, since an onsite inspection following any construction would be mandated. The Township paid for the drawing of the plans and a professional Clerk of the Works. The residents did the construction. The cost to the taxpayers about $35,000. Had the Township bid the project and assumed total responsibility for construction, the pricetag to the taxpayers about $125,000.

I cannot begin to relate in this book the number of drainage-related problems that the Township undertook in my 12 years as Mayor in order to address the needs of the community. Some of the areas included Johnson Road, Whitman Drive, Gardendale, Goodwin Drive, Birches West, Old Birches, Bells Lake Road, Madison Avenue, Cross Keys-Mayfair, Black Horse Pike, Holly Grove Estates, East Holly Avenue, Fish Pond Road, Peach Tree, Twin Ponds East and more. Cost to the taxpayers was in the neighborhood of $4,000,000 to fix what residential developers left us.

Chapter 21

Bonding, Taxes and Abatement

I'm sure, to the average person, municipal financing and accounting seems mundane. At times, given the attention that Council people fail to give to the budget hearings and the monthly bill list, they too find talking money, especially not their own, mundane. The one lesson that politicians need to learn is to speak plainly to the public about spending. The public doesn't need to hear the droning of a Business Manager going through a plethora of budgetary details that are meaningless to the average person. The taxpayer needs to know how much we are spending, in what areas are we spending these dollars, and how does all this affect the taxes? If the budget is increasing, WHY? And please, don't blame the other guy. If the budget is increasing on your watch, it is your responsibility!

Gerald J. Luongo, Ph.D.

Taxes

For years a tax bill, as published by most communities, simply provided the assessed value of the land and the improvements, the rate per $100.00 of assessed value and the total tax being paid. It didn't take me long to realize that this type of tax bill was totally inadequate and the system needed to be changed in order to educate the taxpayer as to how their tax dollars were being spent. I was one of New Jersey's leaders in producing the Educated Consumer's Tax Bill. This was an itemized tax bill that used a bar graph to show the taxpayer the total taxes being assessed and the various agencies to which those tax dollars were being distributed. The municipal government in New Jersey is the tax collector and the distribution service. Various agencies may include County government, the local library, school district, fire district, trash district, health agencies, etc. Along with the amount of taxes paid to these agencies, there was a contact phone number. Who is better informed to explain to the public or to provide printed information for the public's review than the taxing agency? The only person who ever complained about this was the president of the local teachers' union, who insisted that it made the schools look bad since they took the largest portion of the tax bill and that I was ducking my responsibility as Mayor to take the heat for property taxes. Although I don't quite understand his logic, I would say that one of their major responsibilities of a Board of Education is the Annual School Budget. In my opinion, the BOE or its professional financial gurus can address the public more directly on this matter.

PROPERTY TAXES

Property taxes are regressive. It presumes that the greater the value of one's real property, the more that person can afford to pay taxes. In other words, predicated on a parochial view, property equates to wealth. Until this misunderstanding is dispelled once and for all, the system of taxing in New Jersey will never change. To date, only one New Jersey Legislator has come forth with a plan to overhaul the present system. Senator Dick LaRosa was defeated in 1998 and his plan never saw the light of day. In 1999, as an Assemblyman, I attempted to revive his Legislative Bill with some modifications, but I was unsuccessful, as talking taxes or anything to do with changing the system is considered heresy. You soon learn, while seated in the Legislature, that things are not necessarily done for the people, but rather for the party and getting re-elected. I had a short-lived legislative career.

As to budgets, what can an elected leader say to the public? A budget is a complex document that requires understanding and study. To talk about "only the bottom line" is somewhat shortsighted. In a growing community that provides the very best in services and education, the bottom line is going to increase if there is to be progress. No one wants to give up more from their income by paying more taxes. If you are going to be called upon to pay more taxes, perhaps if you understood the reasons for that increase, then your opinion might change. I tried to reduce the Township's budget to very basic terms, by department and by comparison, one year to the next with explanations as to increases and/or decreases. Even with all that clarification, I had

Councilpersons sit there with blank stares on their faces. I would give them the budget weeks in advance and offer my services or the services of the Business Administrator to assist them in understanding the document. I must say that two Councilpersons were completely clueless when it came to Budget 101 or General Mathematics: Ginny Weber and Randee Davidson, and they each had a vote on the manner in which the Township would spend the taxpayers' dollars.

BONDING

Though bonding can be explained in terms easy to understand even by the average layman by drawing analogies, this area is always difficult to explain to someone with a closed mind. Bonding is nothing more that a mortgage, a long-term loan to fund major Township-wide improvements without increasing the tax rate to any major amount in any one given budget year. This averaging out of the repayment period allows present and future residents and businesses to accept a fair share of the loan repayment. To attempt to affect any major improvements by paying for those improvements in one budget year would cause spikes in the tax rate that would cause pandemonium. Such an ill-advised action by the government would be tantamount to paying for a house in one or two years. Most people cannot do that! More so, such thinking is grossly unfair to the present taxpayers since they will bear the brunt of such an action. Bonding enables the tax rate to be stabilized and, given the bond market, interest rates can become very favorable, enabling large amounts to be borrowed at low rates. This kind of thinking compares favorably with refinancing your home when interest rates are in the low single digits. Municipal bonds are tax free and investors scramble to buy them because they are guaranteed. While I led the Township, our bond rating was superior, which enabled us to negotiate low interest rates, favorable repayment periods and above all, make Washington Township bonds most desirable to investors. *Elected leaders who make bonding a negative issue are simply ignorant of the process and the mechanics.*

TAX ABATEMENT

My administration enjoyed many positive editorials locally and throughout the region relative to the Township's tax abatement program. Nevertheless, it was overshadowed by a few elected officials and a gaggle of residents who seemingly could not understand or grasp the basic tenets of the program. Throughout the nation and most assuredly in all business-friendly cities, tax abatement programs are the lifelines for the building of a strong business base in a community. They also encourage already established businesses to remain in a community and to expand their facilities. In the specific case of tax abatement in Washington Township, it's sad to say it but nevertheless true that Councilpersons Ginny Weber, Bob Berry and Joe Yost, along with their cronies, who eventually just became old and annoying, could never get beyond personalities in dealing with tax abatement approvals. Rather than dealing with the significance of the project and the long-term financial commitment that was being made in the Township by the investor, these naysayers reduced everything to personalities. Given this infantile and fatuous behavior, hours of precious time were wasted in speeches, insidious and innocuous statements and imbecilic attempts at humor.

In order for the Mayor to attract business to a community, he/she must become involved with the developer, the proposed business owner and all those who are involved in the decision-making process. Who wants to build in a town where the Mayor is an enigma or who is lacking in intelligence or interpersonal skills? The process established for applying for and for granting tax abatement is carefully scrutinized and held to a critical standard such that the applicants' name could be omitted and the project approved or disapproved only on its merits. Given the negativity and the bad rap that tax abatement received in the Township, the plan needs to be spelled out so people can understand it. In spite of the roadblocks that were placed in our way by a few obtuse Councilpersons, my Administration has the distinction of attracting more businesses to the area than any other community in the County. During my 12-year tenure as Mayor, the net worth of Washington Township's ratables was number one, while the tax rate remained one of the lower in the County. That is simply good business sense at work!

The Program and the Process

Step One in the process is completing an extensive application. The application is submitted to the town's certified tax assessor who, after inspecting the application, either rejects or accepts the application as meeting the standard set forth by the Council as outlined in the appropriate enabling Ordinance. Only accepted applications move on to the next step. **Step Two** involves an interview before the Tax Abatement Committee, which is compromised of local businessmen appointed by Mayor and Council. **Step Three** is a recommendation from the Tax Abatement Committee to Council or a rejection of the application. **Step Four** is a presentation of the recommended application before Council by the Tax Abatement Committee. To approve the application, a majority vote of Council is required (three "yes" votes).

THE ABATEMENT PLAN

The Abatement Plan has a financial component and it operates in the following way depending on the total cost of the project, the Abatement Plan is either a three-year or five-year program. The Abatement Plan is only for the IMPROVEMENTS to the land. There is NO TAX ABATEMENT for the land and full taxes are required to be paid in full each year. Any delinquency in paying the property taxes results in the Tax Abatement Approval being rescinded. It is important to note that the land or property is re-zoned to an industrial or commercial rating, therefore increasing the amount of property taxes received by the Township. The abatement is applied only to the improvements on the property based upon the following scale: Three-Year Plan: Year 1=33%, Year 2=66% and Year 3 and beyond=100% of the assessed value of the improvements. Five-Year Plan: Year 1=20%, Year 2=40%, Year 3=60%, Year 4=80% and Year 5 and beyond 100% of the assessed value of the improvements.

CONCLUSIONS ON ABATEMENT

The program is quite forthright and easy to understand when viewed objectively. It's clear that the Mayor is NOT involved in any aspect of the process and therefore his relationship with a developer or investor is totally inconsequential. There is no hidden agenda! I am very confident in saying that my administration's record of attracting retail and non-retail business to this area will never be replicated. This accomplishment is due to a business-friendly posture and my total commitment in seeking out businesses and convincing them to come and grow with us. Many of the projects that I introduced to the Township have reached fruition during 2001-2004 and perhaps even beyond. I did the job that I promised in filling empty stores and bringing new and lucrative businesses to this community. I must comment on the fact that Councilpersons and the public alike seemingly took issue with local businesspersons who applied for tax abatement, but these very same people never questioned outsiders whose names were totally unfamiliar to them. Think for a moment just how convoluted that thinking is: a local businessman who lives in the community, owns a home and other property here, has decided to raise a family here and pays taxes (more than most residents), is treated with disdain because he knows the Mayor. Of course he knows the Mayor, and so do thousands of other people. So the few simple-minded Councilpersons and those of the public who believe in them, think the worst: "He is getting something for nothing." Well, here is a news flash for all of you—all things being equal and you are willing to risk your money in a major venture, you too would qualify for tax abatement, regardless of your relationship with the Mayor. The Mayor is not involved in the process!

ACCOUNTANTS

Regardless how politically obvious the appointment of an accountant is to a municipality, it seems as though the press and the people make a big deal of the accountant's recommendations predicated upon the annual audit. The appointing of an auditor (accountant) is the responsibility of Council and requires a majority vote. As the political balance changes on Council, so does the auditor. You can always tell who will be the next auditor by looking at the campaign filings. Whichever accountant is the most generous to the candidates will have the job. No mystery there. As to the audit recommendations, that too is political. If the Mayor and Council are of opposing parties, the audit will reveal more recommendations and critical comments. If the Mayor and Council are of the same party, the audit will be glowing. The Mayor appoints the Business Administrator and therefore is responsible for the financial operations of the Township under this form of government. Now don't get me wrong, the accountant is not dishonest. Rather, he/she is selective. Accountants can highlight the most minor problems that have absolutely nothing to do whatsoever relative to the integrity or procedures implemented, spending or the collecting of taxes and their appropriate accounting or the personnel responsible for the financial operations of the community. Government operates within a balanced budget and all dollars are accounted for without exception. So for the record, don't put too much stock in an auditor's report. Whoever hires that auditor and pays his/her salary will determine which political party gets the credit or the blame for the end-of-year audit. If something is really awry in the audit, the State will be notified and decisive action taken.

FACTS AND FIGURES

Here is some information that you will never read about in the press (information current as of 2000) in which I take great pride:

- Township's total property value: $2,204,860,300 and in 2nd Place Deptford Township: $1,356,124,900.

- There are 1,683 commercial units, 90% of them occupied. In 1989 only 40% were occupied.

- Total residential units (no apartments) 12,269.

LAND FACTS

- Total area: 23 sq. miles or 14,770 acres

- Rural farmland: 970 acres

- Other open land: 850 acres

- Township-owned open space: 1660 acres

- School land/preservation: 1585 acres

- Total open space: 34%

- Total built out: 66%

- Persons per square mile: 2,022

- Tax Rate Review (increase or decrease noted in cents)

1990	(.10 reduction)
1991	(.02 reduction)
1992	.06 increase
1993:	(.02 reduction)
1994	.10 increase
1995:	.00
1996:	.00
1997:	.09 increase
1998:	.00
1999:	(.04 reduction)
2000:	(.01 reduction)

Average increase over an 11-year period is .013 cents per year. That is only 1.3 cents per year, on the average.

AREAS OF MAJOR EXPENDITURES 1989-2000

- Parks and Recreation: $ 9,912,522

- Affordable Housing: $ 7,194,000

- Land and Buildings: $ 6,529,820

- Road Improvements: $ 6,523,302

- Sanitary Sewers: $ 3,624,799

- Drainage: $ 1,981,494

- Equipment: $ 1,334,143

HONORABLE MENTIONS

- Washington Lake Park voted New Jersey's Park of the Year in 1996 and 1998 and South Jersey's Best Park.

- Voted as one of the Top Ten Communities in which to live.

- Award Best Homes in South Jersey 1995, 1997, 1998, 2000.

- State Model for an Affordable Housing Plan.

- Recreation program staffed by volunteers that served over 8500 children in the community.

- Comprehensive retail shopping and numerous family oriented entertainment facilities.

- Restaurants for every taste and for every budget.

- The WLP Amphitheatre selected as New Jersey's Project of the Year in 2000.

Chapter 22

THE FREEHOLDERS "TRASH" US

I am opposed to "big" government. I have very strong opinions about the size of the federal government which, for all intents and purposes, is too big and most assuredly is inefficient. In the eyes of most political animals, size equates to power. The more you have the government do, the more power they amass. Once given that power, it is virtually impossible to wrestle it back into the hands of the people.

There are specific areas of County government that are totally unnecessary. This additional layer of government is, more times that not, a sea of political patronage jobs, duplicating what is already being accomplished at the local level in a more cost-efficient fashion and with much more accountability. County government's principal role, in theory, is to provide services that local communities are not equipped to offer, due to a lack of funds, facilities and/or personnel. County government is to act as a coordinator in effecting inter-governmental projects with the goal of reducing costs and thus saving the taxpayers' dollars.

Regrettably, in Gloucester County as well as in other New Jersey counties, the temptation of the governing body overseeing County operations to acquire power and to build political empires was so great as to corrupt what could have been an excellent resource for local government officials and the people. At this point in the 21st century, State and County governments are growing and becoming even more bureaucratic. In order to stop, or at least streamline, County or State government would require major surgery. Numerous studies have proven, without exception, that private enterprise or corporate America would face certain bankruptcy if they operated in the same manner as government. From Washington down to the local level, *we have too much government!* On this specific issue, the Libertarian Party is right on target! The average county resident doesn't even know what a freeholder or county commissioner does. In a phrase, "the freeholders or county commissioners operate unabated runaway government at the County level."

The State of New Jersey created the perfect opportunity for County government to extract even more dollars from local taxpayers unnecessarily when it mandated that all 21 New Jersey counties to deal with the problem of waste (trash) management. This State-mandated reform was a result of the environmental lobby that attacked the proliferation of unlicensed, uninspected and abandoned landfills that became too commonplace, endangering the public's health. In mandating such an action, all communities were directed to

use a County-controlled landfill. The ability for a local municipality to bid and negotiate for the removal of its residential trash was virtually eliminated. Free enterprise was
stopped dead in its tracks. In this sweeping State reform, the
Legislature established very few parameters to control the
type of facility, the cost, number of employees, etc. County
government could now bond to build a facility and create
whatever it deemed necessary to staff and operate a County-
controlled landfill, placing TWO burdens squarely on the
shoulders of the taxpayer: *the cost of repaying the bond and
the cost of trash disposal.* This awesome financial burden that
was placed on local government and its people was unfair!
Taxes needed to be increased or programs needed to be cut
at the local level in order to pay what the County deemed
"each municipality's fair share."

Every town is responsible for collecting its own trash
and recyclables either through the local department of public works or by a contracted private vendor. Every town was
further required to utilize the landfill provided by the County
and had no control over the cost. Although cost savings could
be realized by taking the trash out of area to licensed facilities, the Freeholders/Commissioners, with the law on their
side, had the only game in town and they used that game to
extort tax dollars from every town. The Gloucester County
Improvement Authority was charging at least *40% more per
ton* to dispose of trash than the average cost established by
private licensed landfills and trash to steam facilities. Why
was the Gloucester County landfill program so expensive?
Why did the GCIA have the most heavily indebted facility in

New Jersey? Why did the GCIA have more employees and professionals on the payroll than any other County-operated landfill in the State? Why did the Freeholders permit the GCIA carte blanche on the hiring of so many staff and professional employees with unprecedented salaries and benefit packages? Where were Ginny Weber, Steve Sweeney and Bob Smith, the self-proclaimed guardians of the taxpayers' dollars during all this? Why did these high-profile Freeholders at the time permit the raiding of municipal tax dollars to continue, unabated and worse yet, to defend the GCIA in public and praise them for a "job well done"? The answer is quite simple: politics before the people, and patronage to the loyal party members. This power converted into big dollars for the politicians at the taxpayers' expense. Sweeney and Smith didn't become Senator and Assemblyman respectively for their leadership ability, their outstanding service to the people, or their creative and innovative ideas. No, they know how to work the system to their own benefit and have been fooling the people for a quite a long time. But then again in a County that votes Democrat no matter who the candidate may be, these two career politicians must be given credit for playing the game so well. Sweeney and Smith—they are truly political opportunists!

While serving in the State Legislature, I became very involved with Assemblyman John Rooney, who chaired the State Committee that was investigating the County solid waste debacle. I attended every hearing on this issue and had the opportunity to research the operations and budget reports of every County operated solid waste facility in the State.

Gloucester County, far from the largest and most populated County in the State, had the dubious honor of having the largest bonded debt, the greatest number of non-professional and professional employees and appointees, and the highest salaries and most expensive health benefits packages on the aggregate. Also, the per-ton cost of disposal to the taxpayer was in the TOP FIVE COUNTIES in the State! This was a disgrace, totally unacceptable and without any reasonable explanation! Short of holding a gun to the taxpayer's head, the GCIA and the Freeholders were committing armed robbery and getting away with it. Even if I were to be a committee of one, I made the conscious decision to challenge the Freeholders, the GCIA, and "Boss" Sweeney, knowing full well that I was treading on very dangerous ground.

Although it took a great deal of effort and subterfuge, I was able to obtain an unredacted (uncensored) copy of the State's audit of the Gloucester County Improvement Authority's operations. And let me tell you, it was not a pretty sight. Too many people were lining their pockets with hard-earned taxpayer dollars. At this point it was evident that the County Freeholders and the GCIA had to be held accountable for this irresponsible use of taxpayer dollars.

On the subject of this unadulterated budget review, I must share some information which I will do without breaching the confidentiality of my source. I was a Republican legislator in a Republican majority with a Republican Governor, Christine Todd Whitman. It seemed as though the budget review of the GCIA was taking more time than usual. One afternoon, I visited the Governor's Office and I requested a copy of the GCIA audit. I was sent to the Office of Budget and Finance and was told then that the audit was not completed. When I pressed the issue, I was told that the audit committee needed to meet with the GCIA to discuss its findings, after which a final audit would be made available. In other words, the taxpaying public would get the homogenized version of the audit, not the facts as they really were.

I couldn't believe that this was happening, especially after all the scandal about the GCIA appeared in local newspapers. I reached out to my good friend Senator John Matheussen, who met me in the finance office and supported my position to have a unadulterated copy of the GCIA's audit. He too was given a song and dance! Upon returning from lunch, I stopped at my mailbox in the Assembly Majority Caucus Room on my way back to the Township. There among the copious amounts of mail that one receives daily, I came upon a plain brown envelope that contained the unredacted audit of the GCIA. I leafed through it, but realized that I would need to study the document carefully, so I packed up my briefcase, made my way to the parking garage and began my hour drive back to the Municipal Building.

Just as I merged on to 295 South, my secretary, Betty Bartkovsky, called to tell me that both Freeholder Director Sweeney and Senator Zane had called and indicated that they had to speak to me immediately. Did these two powerful Democrats know that I had the audit? If so, how did they find out so soon? In the State's Republican administration, was there someone protecting this Authority who needed to be held accountable? Did I go too far and if so, what would be the cost for my boldness? I decided that I would call when I returned to the Mayor's Office. I was right on target! Both men were angry that I had the temerity to do this and asked what was I going to do with the information. I told them that they would have to wait and see, but I was not going to bury the truth. I was told in no uncertain terms and with the use of several colorful and descriptive adjectives that a price would be extracted for my actions if they got caught in the crossfire.

(Relative to former Senator Raymond Zane, I always respected him for his leadership and intellectual acumen. Although we had a falling out in my first year as Mayor [1989] when I was the first Gloucester County Mayor to support Rob Andrews for Congress and not him, that dissonance was short lived. Frankly I don't know why he got involved with Steve Sweeney and the GCIA because this was not any of his doing. When I was a Democrat, I walked and knocked on doors with his son Ray, Jr., another fine upstanding man whom I admire for his character and integrity, and Steve Sweeney when they ran for Freeholder. Sweeney won because of the Zane association. Little did father and son Zane know that when it came time, Boss Sweeney would do everything in his power to crush these two men in order to reach his own political goals and to advance his personal agenda. In this situation, Sweeney stopped at nothing to eradicate the Zanes from politics. Sad to say, he was successful.)

I brought this entire issue of the GCIA and the cost for disposal to the attention of the 24 mayors in Gloucester County through the appropriate forum of the Gloucester County Mayor's Association, of which I was president. When my fellow mayors realized that landfills out of the county were charging as much as $25.00 less per ton, they were concerned. Depending upon the amount of tonnage, these lower prices could save thousands of dollars per year in disposal costs. In the largest community, Washington Township, the average savings per taxpayer was projected at $120.00 per year or a reduction in the overall Township budget of $1,800,000.00! Coupled with my administration's innovative plan where farmers paid the Township for its leaves and brush, which they composted and sold for a profit, I was able to reduce taxes, hold the line on spending and enable the government to provide more services and facilities for the public. This was a win-win plan for the taxpayers and I was proud of it!

At first, all 24 mayors basically agreed to seek bids out of county, for solid waste disposal. We saw bids as low as $39.50 per ton upwards to $57.50 per ton, but none compared to the $65 to $75 per ton charged by the GCIA. This period of enlightenment was short lived once Boss Sweeney began to bully the mayors one by one. Unlike Washington Township, too many mayors could not afford to buck Sweeney, or perhaps essential services provided for their community by the County would mysteriously be reduced or disappear. The political climate of the County was in the Democrats' favor and these fellow mayors had to live with their party. By January of 1999 all but five mayors had acquiesced to Boss Sweeney and to the Freeholders. I simply refused to acquiesce and contracted our solid waste disposal out of county for $42 a ton, a savings of $23 per ton as compared to the

GCIA's going rate. I however had the difference in the price invested in an interest-bearing account in preparation for a legal opinion not yet rendered by the State's Supreme Court or a lawsuit that might be initiated by the Freeholders against Washington Township. As time would show, the Freeholders got lucky and the money fell from the sky!

No question about it, Steve Sweeney was angry with me. His rude phone calls, the lack of response to me from County Offices about delays or the absence of services paid for by the Township to the County, the constant barrage of negativity at public meetings orchestrated by the Democratic Party, the appearance of a County political appointee, Kenny Gwertz, at Township meetings badgering the Township's Public Works Director, Jim McKeever, and the use of County officials to harass individuals requiring County approvals perceived as a friend of Mayor Luongo. All this was a precursor as to the price that would be extracted from me by Steve Sweeney and his cronies.

On the day of the Township's Reorganization in 1999, at which time the three new Democrat Councilpersons—Lyons, Rapposelli and Davidson—were sworn into office, I gave my annual State of the Township Address. My direct attack on the Freeholders for their blatant arrogance and totally unprecedented dismissal of the State's audit of the operations of the GCIA as "political" did not sit well with Bob Smith or Steve Sweeney. Following the ceremony an angry, red-faced and almost out-of-control Sweeney got in my face and with finger-pointing gestures told me that he would personally get even with me and that he would even the score, no matter what it would take. "You won't be here two years from now," he barked. And guess what? He was right!

In 2000, the Democrat-controlled Council voting along party lines, released every penny held in escrow from the solid waste disposal issue to the Freeholders. The three Democrats obeyed Boss Sweeney and without a whimper, a word of opposition or a concern for the people, the money was released and it was manna from the sky for the Freeholders. No question about it, Sweeney was the piper and the Council danced to his tune! For the record, Councilmen Sam Hart and John Szczerbinski didn't dance and voted NO.

The Council of 1999-2000 was most difficult to work with. I have never worked with three more difficult, disagreeable and disingenuous people in my entire life in any job. They thought nothing of using people for their own political agenda. They would sue just about anyone about anything, thus encumbering expensive settlements and legal fees to prove a point, a point that always proved them WRONG! They would spend taxpayer dollars to humor themselves and yet refuse to allocate money for many projects that were good for the people and for the image of this community. Truly their service cannot help but be regarded as a failure in this community's history.

In Chapter XXV, I will address my issues with the press. At this point, however, it is important to share with the reader the situation with the press and the unredacted audit of the GCIA. *The Gloucester County Times* is a major newspaper in the County and had every reason to do some investigative reporting about the GCIA. There was one reporter at the *Times* who has subsequently resigned. He was very interested in the GCIA and I trusted him and shared the audit with him. He reported back to me that he could not print the information "as is" because the position of the *Times* was that the GCIA should have the opportunity to address the audit. When the story did appear and the homogenized audit was disclosed, Director Dave Shields and the Freeholders simply played down the significance of the audit and, frankly, any stories after that were meaningless. The *Times* missed a golden opportunity to expose the operations of the GCIA.)

Chapter 23

THE AFFORDABLE HOUSING PLAN: A MODEL FOR THE STATE

No matter how hard you try sometimes, something good and positive can be twisted into something negative. Misunderstanding, lies, innuendo, gossip and jealousy are the progenitor of this ugliness. Only the truth can right the wrong. Only the facts can set the record straight. The intelligent reader who seeks the truth will sort the fact from the fiction and draw his/her own conclusions. As to the others, you need to ask yourself, "Do they really care?"

In the early 1970's, the State Supreme Court made history when it upheld the right of all residents in the State of New Jersey to live anywhere they choose. The famed Mount Laurel decision (Mount Laurel, New Jersey) was the first step in yet another program advanced by the Democrats that attempted to deal with changing society. This social experiment, with all its detractors, is the law. Basically what the law states is that the community has the responsibility to provide adequate, suitable and unidentifiable affordable housing to anyone who qualifies under the COAH (Council on Affordable Housing) program. This law prevents communities from discriminating against people who cannot afford the cost of the available housing in a specific community. There is no way of sidestepping the law! Washington Township ignored the law for over 15 years based on the misunderstanding that COAH didn't have the teeth to do anything to enforce the mandate. COAH had the courts on their side and, contrary to the legal opinions of the late John Trimble, Sr. (Washington Township's Solicitor in the 1980's), a town could be forced under the law to provide affordable housing. (Mr. Trimble was the solicitor for Mt. Laurel when the case was argued. It would appear as though he lost the case since he argued against the Affordable Housing mandate. Although he may have been knowledgable about the law, I sincerely question his ability to be objective when advising Washington Township on the matter in the 1980's.)

When I was elected Mayor in 1989, I inherited the unresolved affordable housing program. Of course, due to the previous Council's lack of action on this matter, the Township was under the direction of the Court to take action, and not COAH. We were almost in contempt of Court and the Court Master appointed by the Judge to oversee the town's progress wanted to know what we would do. There was no easy solution. Since 1975 through 1988, SIXTY-NINE approvals for residential housing units were approved, representing 12,325 living units (includes apartments, condominiums, town houses and single-family homes). If Council had taken the time to realize that only 398 units had to be "affordable," they could have been so designated in the Town's Master Plan and the matter would have been addressed in an equitable solution. They chose to ignore COAH, based upon faulty legal advice.

To further complicate the matter, the Township had three lawsuits pending that charged the Planning Board and the Township Council with denying three developers the right to construct residential units because they included affordable housing units. The affordable housing matter was exacerbated with the approval of 1380 residential units prior to the 1990 moratorium on building (Led by Council President John Rogale, Council adopted an ordinance that stated that the MUA was unable to provide sufficient water for further development.) and the implementing of my ordinance adopted by Council that restricted homes ONE to the acre on the aggregate. COAH provides that affordable housing can be constructed on any property regardless of zoning and the lot size will permit about six residential units to the acre. Additionally, the "developer's remedy" provides the builder the right to include non-inclusive (regular housing) housing units based upon the ratio ONE affordable housing unit to every FOUR non-inclusive housing units. This community could not absorb this kind of residential impact considering the collateral consequence that such an influx of people would have on the municipality's services and the schools. Also of major concern was the fact that the Township's approved

Affordable Housing Plan identified 13 sites throughout the Township that included prime commercial, light industrial, institutional and planned recreational parcels. This was not good! The plan had to be revised! The question was how?

One of the plans put forth by the Council and rallied behind by several residents was to identify areas of the Township already constructed and occupied. Within those developments, based upon resale value and the condition of the home and the neighborhood, certain living units could be identified as "affordable." In my opinion, this wasn't fair to the homeowner or to the neighbors. After all, at the time of occupancy the site was not part of an Affordable Housing Plan and such information may have affected the prospective buyer's decision to purchase. Also, the present occupants may not qualify for such housing under the income guidelines established by COAH. And finally, the sections of the community that Council and the resident wanted to identify as affordable had already been labeled unfairly and we as a community needed to be inclusive, not exclusive and divisive. I knew that I needed more information to address this program and, frankly, I wasn't happy with the answers I was getting from the Planner and the Township's solicitor. It was time to do my own research!

I met with the Court Master and members of COAH and found them to be quite receptive in providing assistance, especially when I demonstrated my sincerity in having the Township do its part to resolve the Affordable Housing mandate in an efficient, thorough and expedient fashion. A plan could be redrafted, but I was made to understand that the Court

Master and COAH would need to work with me every step of the way and that any recommendations to Council or the Planning Board had to meet with their approval. Also, I had to meet with the three developers who had the unresolved lawsuits and get them to agree to the plan. And finally, the entire plan would need to be presented before a Superior Court Judge for his/her approval. This was not an easy task, but I was ready for the challenge!

What did other communities and cities do about the Affordable Housing mandate? As a member of the New Jersey Conference of Mayors, I could research this question quite easily by speaking with the mayors directly or the persons in charge of Housing and Urban Development. The advice from all mayors who had a successful Affordable Housing Program was to include in the developmental stages a developer who was an authority on the subject. We were quite fortunate to have in our immediate area Brad Ingerman of Cherry Hill, New Jersey. The affordable housing developments that he planned were models throughout the State and the country. When I presented his name to the Court Master and COAH as the person who I would like to advise me in the developing of a plan, they embraced the selection.

The first order of business was to establish the objectives of the plan, ensuring compliance with the Courts mandate:

1. Reduce the number of required affordable units by developing Regional Contribution Agreements with communities within our region.

2. Establish a need for affordable senior housing that would also provide us with COAH credits.

3. Provide a recreational component for any affordable housing site that was non-inclusive.

4. Settle the outstanding developers' lawsuits without building more homes.

5. Reduce the number of identified sites from 13 to 2, thus eliminating the potential for residential overdevelopment and the loss of prime real estate.

This plan was approved by the Court Master and COAH. I was now ready to make a presentation to the Planning and Zoning Boards, Council and the public. Three meetings were scheduled, the plan was reviewed in detail, the sites identified, all costs clearly spelled out and every question answered. Simultaneously, I was meeting with the three developers and their attorneys with the goal of convincing them to withdraw their lawsuits. They accepted the plan and the lawsuits were withdrawn. (As an example of what could have been, a shopping center was planned for the property directly across the street from the Chestnut Ridge Middle School.)

The night of the final adoption of the Affordable Housing Master Plan Ordinance, there was absolutely no objection and the ordinance passed 5-0. The Affordable Housing Plan was presented to the Court Master and COAH. They accepted the plan and the next step was a court hearing before Judge Francis of the Superior Court. Every detail of the plan was made public and informational packets were made available to the public and the press. Judge Francis, after a hearing,

Police Chief Giordano and Mayor Luongo following a visit by Governor Christine Todd Whitman. (Looking on Corporal Tim Attanasi.)

The Assemblyman visits one of the many medical facilities in the 4th Legislative District of New Jersey.

The Fire Department demonstrates new equipment purchased under a State of New Jersey Grant sponsored by Assemblymen Luongo and Geist and Senator Matheussen.

The Assembly Office Staff saying "hello." (l-r) Jacqui Lauletta & grandkids, Fran Capetola, the Assemblyman, and Arthur Capetola.

One of our volunteers, Erna Huber, takes care of our public information table at one of many community events.

With the votes tabulated, the newly elected Assemblyman Luongo addresses a legion of workers and supporters.

Recognizing Personal Achievement

Mayor and Assemblyman Luongo recognizing a Student of the Month at the Bell's School, along with the proud mother.

"We must continue to recognize and reward outstanding teachers and administrators. They make all the difference in public education."
Assemblyman Gerald J. Luongo

Chief Sowney (l) and Mayor Luongo swear in new police officers.

Mayor Luongo welcomes The Special Olympics to Washington Lake Park.

Assemblyman Luongo publicly supports the FOP and PBA. The Assemblyman's youngest son Matthew (l) a Sergeant with the Delaware River Port Authority Police Department and Police Chief Edmund Giordano (r) look on.

One of many happy seniors playing a rubber of bridge at the township's Senior Center.

Regular visits to nursing homes keeps the Assemblyman informed about the needs of the elderly. A community volunteer, Roseann Lafferty, looks on.

Comedian and Performer Cozy Morley, the Mayor and President of the Senior Citizen's Committee, Tom Donahue, take a break from a Senior Citizens Spring Gala at the Center.

William Kettleson, Government Relations Director for ComCast and Mayor Luongo proudly display their respective awards from the New Jersey Conference of Mayors at the NJCM Annual Awards Dinner at the Taj Mahal in Atlantic City, NJ.

Public service can be very rewarding. Mayor Luongo being recognized as New Jersey's Mayor of the Year!

Truly Concerned About Senior Citizens

The Senior Center of Washington Township provides a beautiful center where all seniors can gather in friendship and enjoy numerous activities.

A 100th Birthday! Now that's one heck of an accomplishment!

Just one of many Town Meetings and one of the many folks who need a question answered.
(Police Chief Will Sowney to the (r) of the Mayor/Assemblyman.)

approved the plan. I had done due diligence and, as directed from the very outset of this venture, was extremely careful in every step that I took. I did what was right for the people!

The Affordable Housing Plan as approved by the Superior Court of New Jersey (abridged version):

1. Total number of units required to be built in Washington Township: 191.

2. Site ONE, County House Road, 96 units with a recreational component (Township soccer complex, playground and walking/jogging trail). No non-inclusive housing.

3. Site TWO, Sawyers Creek with 95 units (condos) with non-inclusive residential homes.

4. Hunter Chase, American Newlands and Sheffield Gate lawsuits settled.

5. Under a Regional Contribution Agreement, Gloucester City and Camden received a total of $3,000,000.

6. The Township committed $370,000 to housing rehabilitation in the community.

7. In lieu of building additional homes, $3,440,000 in credits to Sawyers Creek, American Newlands and County House Road developers.

8. Independent appraisal by an approved and certified land appraiser for the purchase of open space for community use at County House Village, $384,000.

9. The preservation of precious open space.

10. **Total cost = $7,194,000.**

The thinking behind this plan was to reduce residential growth and to reduce the potential number of children that could enter the school district. The old plan would have produced at least 3,500 residential units yielding, on average, 1.5 children per unit. Based upon the average school enrollment growth of 2% per year, we did the math:

- 3500 homes x 1.5 children = 5250 children

- 5250 x 12 years x $7000.00 per year = $ 431,000,000

This program was another win-win for the Township. The program served the needs of the people while meeting the mandate of the Court and the Affordable Housing Law. I could never figure out why some people found fault with the program. Perhaps they are the same people who find fault with everything else.

As I reflect upon the events that were precipitated by a article on the County House Road Land acquisition that appeared in the *Philadelphia Inquirer* on June 16, 1999, I am perplexed how anyone could accept that article as anything but malicious fiction. The facts were carefully buried under a mound of innuendo and conjecture, woven into carefully worded sentences that strung together unrelated and inconsequential events, places people and occurrences that were only given credence by comments made from uninformed, reckless, irresponsible and politically motivated individuals. The absence of any comments about the contracts relative to the Regional Contribution Agreement, Sawyers Creek or American Newlands, substantiates my allegations that this was a hate article which reeked of yellow journalism at its worst. Furthermore, I faced a packed Council room two weeks later with incontrovertible facts and the documents to prove what I was saying to be the absolute truth. I answered every question addressed to me. I responded to the questions and to the innuendo and insults of attorneys Jack and John Trimble, who I disarmed and put in their place with the truth. I watched the reporter Maureen Graham, who wrote the story, ignore what I had to say at the meeting. She stood in the back of the room, totally unabashed, talking with Randee Davidson and other political cronies. The lack of a substantial story in the *Inquirer* the next day was proof positive that she had no intention of ever printing the truth.

Let me conclude a well-deserved critical analysis of Graham by telling a story which will prove my point that her contempt towards me and many of my supporters has prevented her from ever writing a fair and impartial story. After the June 16th story appeared in the paper, I was absolutely taken aback and had no idea what this was all about. Mr. Alacqua, solicitor for the Township, arranged a conference call with Brad Ingerman, Judge Francis, Maureen Graham and me. In the course of that discussion, every question that she asked was answered. Not one of us could understand where she was coming from—she was way off base. I asked her where she had been for the 18 months that we were working on this plan in full view of the public. The final comment from Judge Francis will always remain with me and provides me solace: *"Ms. Graham, you don't seem to be interested in the facts or the truth. I am sure that you will write whatever you want, so go write your story."*

Graham needed no encouragement from the judge. She always wrote what she *thought* were the facts and, if proven wrong, she never quite corrected her fictional stories. And as to her publisher, the *Inquirer,* I believe their motto should be "Sales over substance." Often sued for inaccuracies and notoriously incorrect information printed as fact, the deep pockets of the *Inquirer* have enabled them to scare off potential lawsuits from those of us who simply don't have the money to go the distance.

Chapter 24

THE JUDICIARY COMMITTEE: POLICE, POLITICS AND POWER

I truly respect many members of the Washington Township Police Department and to this day, hold them in high regard. Although many of the rank-and-file officers were driven into relative silence and seclusion during the menacing, Machiavellian and dictatorial reign of Chief Francis Burke, I still believe that these men and woman respect what I did for the department. The appointment of my friend Chuck Billingham as Police Chief in 2004 will provide the leadership needed to breathe life back into this department and bring about a renaissance that will see a vast improvement in morale and the attitude of the men and women in blue.

As I reflect upon the names of those whose careers I was able to jump-start, I realize that it must have been very difficult for them to try and go through their daily routine when there were cowards in the department with entirely too much time on their hands. These are the "coward cops" who fax to the press and/or post unsigned letters critical of the Mayor or his allies, derogatory comments and cartoons about others and of course, mocking the officers who were labeled "Jerry's kids." Of course, none of these cowards have the character or integrity to come forward. No, they hid in the shadows, lurking like a thief in the night. I can understand an officer denying any friendship with me just to be left alone. But then again, many have stood up to Burke and his thugs and these officers took a hit. They got knocked down, but they didn't get knocked out—they rose to the occasion and stood tall. When put to that kind of test and you stand tall, that is called character. Of course there are the few who aligned themselves with a man like Burke because either they are cut from the same cloth or they permitted themselves to be intimidated. I believe that history will prove me 100% correct when I state that the department under Francis Burke will be regarded as the darkest period in the history of the Washington Township Police Department.

I want to talk about the superior officers who were led by Francis Burke and Lloyd Dumont, who created the appearance of corruption and incompetent leadership in the department for the sole purpose of providing the Democratic members of Council the excuse to form a Judiciary Committee. This kangaroo court held meetings behind closed doors in order to conduct what was purported to be a non-biased, non-political investigation into the police department, when in fact it was nothing more than a gripe session for the dysfunctional few and a way of smearing the reputations of good people. I'd like to understand how Council President Matthew Lyon, a licensed attorney in the State of New Jersey, could possibly believe that, after all the testimony that was given, that I and/or the public would settle for a final report that consisted of nothing more than hearsay and unsubstantiated allegations. Worse yet, an unredacted copy of the proceedings was never provided. How can an investigating committee call as it principal witnesses the officers who signed a public letter against their boss, Chief Wil Sowney, and reward these officers for violating a policy which they required all other officers to abide by? (Rule 8:1.21 and 8:1.72. as adopted by the Township.) Did every one of the superior officers who signed this letter realize that they were being used to advance the careers of two people, Francis Burke and Lloyd Dumont? The Judiciary Committee states that they withheld the names of four civilians who alleged that they were refused jobs with the police department because they would not pay for them. The conclusion in the report directs them to speak to the appropriate State agency for further investigation. No such agency was ever called, nor was I ever contacted by any such agency. If there were such witnesses, and that is at best doubtful, they lied! This was just another ruse perpetrated by Councilpersons Lyons and Rapposelli, where they would order one of their political cronies to say or sign anything, including lawsuits, in order to make it all look above board to the public. Apparently in making such an allegation, Lyons and Rapposelli missed the class on Constitutional Law, specifically the 6th Amendment to the Constitution of the United States. But then again, they trampled the rights of a lot of people who got in their way.

Beginning in the latter part of 1994, I appointed Captain T. Powers and Captain Jack Wynne to lead the police department on an alternating basis due to the chronic failing health of Chief Richard Moore. This lasted for almost 18 months. Although Powers and Wynne had different styles of leadership, they were both good men and had the department and the community at heart. They did an excellent job and I respect everything that they accomplished in this caretaker role. In January of 1995, Chief Richard Moore died. The department lost a leader who understood the thinking of police officers and most assuredly understood his role vis-à-vis the public. The Township lost a fine man. Knowing only two police chiefs up to that point, Fred Reeves and Rich Moore, I needed someone who emulated their kind of leadership, ability, personality and who understood the importance of working with the political leaders and not against them. Police have a responsibility that far exceeds what is expected from other professionals. Nevertheless, they must answer to a higher authority and in this form of government it is the Mayor who represents the people. I didn't create the law but I was responsible for implementing it. Throughout a respectable period of mourning for Chief Moore, it was rumored that Francis Burke was obviously going to be the next Chief. Personally, I always question the obvious.

Both Captain Wynne and Captain Powers indicated that they would be retiring and were not interested in the position. The position was then posted, applications were received and reviewed, and an interview schedule posted. Every interview was tape recorded. Council people were invited to the interviews and to ask questions. The final decision as to the selection of a Chief of Police lies solely with the Mayor. (In 2000, Councilpersons Lyons, Rapposelli and Davidson challenged this authority. In 2001 the Superior Court of New Jersey upheld the authority of the Mayor to make such appointments, striking down the lawsuit of the three Councilpersons mentioned. In the latter part of 2001, Council took action to diminish the responsibilities of a floundering Mayor Davidson by appointing itself as the Director of Public Safety, which in essence provided them authority over the Chief of Police and subsequently the police department. I believe that action to be illegal.)

There were some excellent candidates, many of whom could lead the department. Least impressive was Francis Burke, who at the time of the interview was a lieutenant. He was quite fortunate to have benefited from the Township's generous college tuition reimbursement plan and had an impressive college background and several citations for numerous training classes. His sensitivity to my inquiries as to how he managed all the college, training institutes and teaching assignments while working for the Township always elicited a testy response (which became downright ugly when he decided to join forces with Council and get me out of office), leading me to believe that he lacked some very important interpersonal skills necessary for this police department. Francis Burke never said it, but his body language and his responses to my questions clearly indicated that he resented being interviewed by a mere civilian. Burke seemingly was a legend in his own mind and it manifested itself in the way in which he responded to people. In June of 1995, when I appointed Wil Sowney to be Chief and James Murphy, Deputy Chief, I knew that Burke would somehow or other even the score. In my opinion, it wasn't a matter of him not liking me. He never liked me! Burke simply had a problem with my philosophy about local policing. Just because I am not a police officer, doesn't negate the fact that I may have some ideas that could improve police services. I too am educated and have taken the time to read and to do research. I am entitled to an opinion, since it is I that must answer directly to the people.

From June of 1995 until December of 1998, this community was running quite well. The Township Council operated in a professional fashion, making an effort to keep politics out of governing—and it was working. The morale in the police department was especially high and the men and women saw many positive changes under the direction of Chief Sowney and Deputy Chief Murphy. New programs, superior community responses and dialogues with neighborhoods and individuals having problems with specific officers strengthened the image of a caring department in the public's eye. New ideas from the officers were encouraged and in many cases implemented. Officers were respected by the leadership and the collegial relationship among the officers was at an apex. The number of grievances diminished, and those that were filed were handled quickly and fairly. Negotiated contracts were settled in a timely fashion and the relationship between the PBA, FOP, their attorney and the Mayor's Office was at its best. Rules and Regulations were adopted and everything placed into writing to ensure that everyone was held to the same standards, and fairly.

The department grew in terms of new police personnel and we embarked upon a 10-year plan to move forward regardless of the few in the department who could never "get with the program." Both Sowney and Murphy recommended many promotions and developed a new leadership team. I questioned some of those appointments and shared grave concerns about specific promotions. I was told unequivocally that I was wrong and that these men had changed for the better and that they knew what they were doing was best for the department and for the community. Well, unfortunately I was right. I believe that Chief Sowney thought that by promoting and recognizing Fran Burke, Wayne Lanholm, Robert Zbikowski, Lloyd Dumont and Kenneth Condit as part of the "leadership team," somehow or other they would be team players, working with him and Deputy Chief Murphy, in earnest, to improve the quality and delivery of police services in the community. This proved to be a faulty assumption and deleterious to Chief Sowney's future.

Gerald J. Luongo, Ph.D.

THE HONEYMOON IS OVER

The rumblings among the superior officers began to surface when I, as Mayor, began to question some of the actions that had been taken by officers under their command, actions of the detective division or actions of the superior officers as they related to members of the public who had filed complaints. I had over a dozen written complaints from the public that had been, according to the complainants, "swept under the rug by the police department." In my opinion, to receive so many complaints in writing as well as a number of complaints that I received by phone (from people afraid to put anything in writing for fear of reciprocity), I felt that it was in my purview to ask questions. On at least two occasions, the allegations against one of the superior officers were so egregious that I was forced to call in the County Prosecutor's Office. We all met with the resident and, sad to say, the loser in this whole matter was me. The officer lamented that I wasn't supportive and "loyal" to the men in blue, while the resident contended that I was clearly on the side of the police regardless of the facts. The Prosecutor's Office simply took the position that this was a "local matter." Subsequent meetings with other residents and/or the officers and the residents proved to be unproductive. When questioned, the attitude of the officers became pervasive and they objected to "civilians" meddling in police matters. How could I question or doubt the veracity of a police officer in deference to a civilian who had every reason to lie? This is a tenuous position for any elected official! The superior officers

244

regarded this as "meddling" on my part. I think that I was simply doing my job!

The other problem that the superior officers seemed to have was the fashion in which candidates were recommended for officer positions. On the average, between the Chief's Office and the Mayor's Office, some 350 letters requesting applications for a position with the WTPD were received each year. The vast majority of the requests were from certified officers looking for a change in employment, as well as new recruits asking to be sent to the police academy. Many of the certified officers had either superior recommendations or graduated in the top 10% of their class at the academy. Given the Township's minimum requirement of an associate's degree or 60 college credits for hiring, we had many candidates with four-year degrees and more. The selection process was not an easy one.

It was no secret that the Mayor made recommendations to the Chief of Police for those individuals that he would like to see interviewed. In reality, there isn't a police person on the WTPD who wasn't recommended by someone already on the force, a member of the community or an elected official. Given the number of young people who grew up in this community and the number of young people who served as a Police Explorer in the community, there was a wealth of talent right here at home. I knew many of their parents and they reached out to me on behalf of their son or daughter. Many of the kids grew up in my neighborhood or knew my three sons and they too reached out to me. Priests and ministers, teachers and school counselors, administrators and elected officials from our community, as well as other communities, reached out to me, along with officers in our own police department, to hire friends, daughters, sons, sons-in-law, etc. When the superior officers tried to sell the idea that "Mayor Luongo controlled the hiring," they are so wrong, and every officer hired knows that! All things being equal as to qualifications, jobs were given not to strangers but to those candidates who had reputable individuals standing up for them!

In the final analysis, all individuals recommended to the Chief for employment in the department were tested and investigated by officers assigned this responsibility in the police department. If an unqualified person was hired as alleged by the superior officers and echoed by Council in their kangaroo court Investigating Committee, then the assigned investigator failed to do his job effectively and he should be held accountable, not the mayor. Any person deemed "not qualified" was never hired and I never interfered with that decision. Anything said to the contrary is an outright, boldface lie! I could easily demonstrate the inconsistency and the partisan politics played by the superior officers when in fact, prior to the publishing of this book, an officer who I hired and who was a lightning rod for their charges of the "improper hiring of an unqualified individual," was promoted by then Chief Burke. Obviously, I had good judgment!

In retrospect, I surmise that the straw that broke the camel's back was my questioning the manner in which a corporal's test was administered, and the overruling of a superior officer in his decision about demoting and/or dismissing of a subordinate. I did not want to get involved in either of these matters, but the inequities were so blatant that they screamed out to be addressed. I reached out to both Chief Sowney and Deputy Chief Murphy to see if they could resolve the matter by explaining to the parties involved that I had examined the reports of the superior officers and felt their explanation was dubious. The promotional test reeked of favoritism by the use of weighting a subjective interview. The discipline was punitive and an act of retribution. Believe me, those conclusions on my part didn't sit well with the superior officers.

I have no intention of divulging these officers' names since the matter is in the past. I mention it to demonstrate the lack of professionalism among the superior officers who should have set examples of appropriate work ethic, character, integrity, leadership, the giving and the taking of orders and, finally, admitting mistakes and taking responsibility for them. In my opinion, several of the superior officers on the Sowney/Murphy leadership team lacked these professional attributes which I saw clearly when Sowney was trumpeting their promotions, which I reluctantly approved. That one decision that Sowney made, with the support of Murphy, was Sowney's undoing.

Unlike many elected officials, I have always put everything into writing. I believe that if you have something to say, your signature is a validation of your belief and commitment to your position. I object strongly and generally ignore all unsigned correspondence and believe that the press does a disservice to publish unsigned letters. Conversely, the use of informants who remain anonymous or who sell information in exchange for favors is also reprehensible. The point here is that the reaction to my decision on the two matters from one of the superior officers was a comment to Chief Sowney: "Why don't you tell that *dago* Mayor to mind his own f—ing business?" What troubled me in that short but powerful statement was the use of the ethnic slur. That was also the beginning of the attacks from other superior officers and Assemblyman Robert Smith of the 4th District. Was this anger against me from the superior officers about my decision making, or did it have to do with the fact that I was an educated and successful Italian-American?

The Chief Under Siege

(The number of memos, letters and correspondence on the issues to be discussed from this point forward presently occupy four binders representing over THREE FEET of paperwork compiled during a period of 20 months. Also, I have several taped recordings provided me by various members of the police department and the public. All my allegations and conclusions stated herein are predicated on this information. Everything has been properly catalogued into exhibits in the event that I should be called upon to present them in any legal proceedings.)

It is one thing to face your detractors when you know who they are. Its quite another to be blindsided by anonymous accusers which forces you into a state of mind in which you are unable to make these allegations public, but forced to question the loyalty, motives and intentions of all persons—police and civilian, staff officers to line patrolmen. Chief Sowney was about to experience all this, as well as a state of despondency promulgated by hidden accusers with hidden agendas.

This situation began in 1999, shortly after Lyons, Rapposelli and Davidson took office. I will be critical of many people, including the Federal Bureau of Investigation. What was in store for Sowney and for me was carefully orchestrated with the one goal of destroying us. With the help of people thought loyal to us, the subversive conduct of the Democratic majority on Council that desperately wanted the Mayor's Office, the final nails were placed in our respective public service coffins. I have never experienced such baneful behavior on the part of so many people who seemingly disregarded the simple rules of decency in the quest for power!

Although I was not aware of the situation involving Chief Sowney and the FBI until late January of 1999, it was nevertheless the first in a series of attacks that basically debilitated Sowney. On January 25, 1999 Sowney was contacted by Robert Downey, the Chief Resident Agent of the FBI's Cherry Hill Office. He requested a meeting with Sowney for the next day. When Sowney arrived for it, Downey was joined by Special Agents Paul Murray and William Grace. Sowney was advised that he was a target of an investigation as a result of information received from an informant that Sowney was involved in an auto accident while under the influence of alcohol and that he (Sowney) had orchestrated a cover-up.

The accident allegedly occurred in Mantua or Deptford Township and repairs were made at an undisclosed bodyshop with the cost of said repairs being passed on to another vehicle. The FBI refused to divulge the name of the informant and mentioned some nonsense about a process of identifying the informant that took 18 months. (Amazing! The allegations and charges are responded to immediately by the FBI but once proven false, the FBI still protects the identity of the liar. I'm sure that many people would like to know this person's name.) The Chief rightfully stated that this was political, but the FBI was going to investigate it anyway. The Chief was told not to discuss this with anyone!

On January 27, 1999 a memo was slipped under the door of the Internal Affairs office. A patrolman described his conversation with Superior Officer Lieutenant Lloyd Dumont in which Dumont denied anything to do with a "problem that the Chief is having with the FBI." Dumont also stated that "the Police Department has two teams and you want to make sure that you are on the right team." I was still unaware of what was going on until I received a call from Council President Rapposelli, who indicated that he had "information regarding an employee that may require immediate firing." I chose not to meet with Rapposelli but asked him to reduce what he had to tell me into writing. He did so and had the memo hand-delivered to my office on January 28, 1999. I asked Sowney to come to my office immediately. I shared with him the memo, which paralleled the "confidential" discussion that Sowney had with the FBI. To make this entire matter even more bizarre, the memo written by Dumont vehemently denying any involvement in the matter contains the same information. Coincidence or collusion? Do we dare speculate that perhaps Councilman Rapposelli and Lieutenant Dumont orchestrated this entire ruse? Did they dupe the FBI? Were there other police personnel or elected officials involved in this conspiracy? Did someone fabricate information in order to gain status as a FBI informant in exchange for immunity on a pending investigation of which they were a target? Did the FBI breach their confidentiality directive?

We had a patrol officer attempting to get information on what was happening relative to "the Chief's DWI problem." Another officer submitted a memo to the Chief indicating that he was called by Councilwoman Randee Davidson, who told him "to spy on the police department and to provide her with any information by calling her directly." This is a direct violation of the Administrative Code. When I brought this to the attention of Council President Rapposelli, his response was: "Big deal—ask me if I care."

I directed the Chief to meet with Business Administrator MaryAnn Chalow and to provide the FBI the purchase order for the repairs to the Chief's car, the cancelled check and the report that indicated that the car was damaged in the parking lot of the Municipal Building following a meeting in December of 1998. I further directed the Chief to pass along to the FBI the memos from Dumont, Rapposelli and the officer reporting Councilwoman Davidson as well as the memo from another police officer who was being "pressured" to say that he had information about the Chief's alleged DWI. This whole thing smelled of rotten politics and I trusted that the FBI would see this for what it was and take appropriate action against the person(s) making these false allegations. To date, nothing has been done. A man's career was almost ruined by an investigation that continued for months before the FBI would put it to rest. How unfortunate for Wil Sowney.

From the beginning of January 1999 through March 10, 1999, Sowney found it difficult to work with his leadership team because he no longer trusted them. Due to the interference of the Democratic members of Council into the operations of the police department and the turmoil created in the department by Council's minions, it seemed not a day passed without an incident. The final blow was delivered to Sowney on March 11, 1999, when a "Letter of No Confidence" from the superior officers was slipped under his door when he was out of the office for three days. Of course, the letter was faxed to the press on the same day as it was slipped under an empty office door. Talk about cowards! Is this the example that the superior officers were setting for subordinates to emulate?

From this point on until his retirement in the fall of 1999, Sowney became ineffectual. His spirit was broken and he felt betrayed—rightfully so. He was a kind, generous, emotional and sensitive man who cared about people. I don't know of anyone who didn't like Wil Sowney. His detractors used this against him. These people can never be forgiven for what they did to this man. All the hard work that was begun in the summer of 1995 in building the most efficient, effective and harmonious police department in the State began to unravel quickly as the fight for power and control erupted with sides being chosen, lines being etched in the sand and the ugly side of several individuals being exposed in order to curry favor with the Democrat-controlled Council, who took delight in seeing the seeds of their evil deeds erupt into chaos. On April 22, 1999 Council, acting solely on the Letter of No Confidence, initiated a Judiciary Committee to investigate the operations of the Police Department. This of course was a self-fulfilling prophecy and was passed along political lines, with Sam Hart and John Sczcerbinski voting No and Lyons, Rapposelli and Davidson voting Yes. Another victory for the bad guys!

THE JUDICIARY COMMITTEE

As I've said, the Judiciary Committee was the most over-rated bit of political hype that I have ever seen in Washington Township politics. In fact, I'd say it was deja vu of the investigation of former Mayor John Robertson. You cannot create smoke without a fire, so, with the help of the duplicitous superior officers, Council found the fuel to start the fire. Council had found their Brutus, or two or three, who would do anything to get rid of Wil Sowney and Jerry Luongo. These impuissant individuals needed to "get the power" they believed would give them stature among the rank and file, a power that they were unable to earn through hard work and respect from their peers.

Matthew Lyons and Ray Rapposelli orchestrated this Judiciary Committee with help from more cunning individuals. Their single-minded mission was to embarrass and discredit the Mayor and Chief of Police. But in reality, they were *simple minded,* as time would show. There was nothing amiss in the police department and no matter how hard they tried to find something, or in desperation create something, the bottom line read loud and clear: too many superior officers had too much time on their hands with too many personal scores to settle among the rank and file. If Council had approached the Judiciary Committee in earnest, involving me in the process due to my knowledge and expertise in the area of human resources, they would have been able to develop sufficient grounds to dismiss several officers, from all ranks, from the department. Instead, Lyons and Randee Davidson sat there on that Judiciary Committee, spending $6,000 of the taxpayers' money simply to listen to hearsay information from a group of frustrated guys venting their spleens in hopes of currying favor with the Democratic leadership on Council by telling them what they wanted to hear. Do you have any idea as to the total cost paid in salaries, benefits and other perks to the superior officers? As a rough estimate, over $900,000 for SIX officers! In my opinion, their time would be better spent on police work, not politics.

The superior officers lamented to the Judiciary Committee that there were serious problems in the areas of hiring, promotions, assignments, cronyism, discipline, political meddling, inadequate planning and communications. After dissecting the transcript of the Judiciary Committee, I have the following questions and concerns:

1. The superior officers boasted that each one of them had over 20 years of experience, yet, to the best of my knowledge, not one of them could point to a single accomplishment in all those 20 years that would define them as an exceptional law enforcement officer.

2. In the 12 years that I sat in the Mayor's chair, I cannot point to even one piece of correspondence that brings up any of the concerns that prompted their Letter of No Confidence.

3. Other than the opinions of the superior officers, there is not one single piece of documentation to support any of their claims.

4. The basis of what was stated as "fact" by several of the superior officers was only hearsay, based upon third-party information and, in a court of law, inadmissible because such statements cannot be corroborated.

5. If the superior officers were such exceptional leaders, as they state, then as part of the leadership team, why didn't they make any meaningful contributions to the police department?

6. Other than complaining and griping about other officers and their lack of performance, not one superior officer can point to any constructive program of self-improvement that was provided for an underachieving officer in the department.

7. Did the superior officers have their feathers ruffled when I suggested weekend shifts and/or more visibility during patrol shifts other than 8 a.m. to 4 p.m. weekdays?

8. Although it is true that the Chief of Police appoints superior officers, are these men so naive to believe that any Chief takes such action without communicating with the Mayor to sign off on such actions?

9. Based upon their personal record of achievement, how can the superior officers who signed the Letter of No Confidence in Chief Sowney state unequivocally that they "deserved to be promoted"? They accused me of being delusional when I refuted that faulty, self-serving conclusion on their part.

10. If the Judiciary Committee had provided the same anonymity to the rank-and-file officers as they did to the mysterious, unidentified residents who spoke against the Mayor, I'm sure that the Judiciary Committee would have had a different opinion as to the credibility of the superior officers. Of course, that assumes that the Judiciary Committee was interested in the truth!

11. The Judiciary Committee chose to include a statement from Captain Wayne Lanholm as fact when he stated; "I was talking to Councilwoman Ginny Weber and she told me that anyone that wanted to be a police officer had to pay $3500 and it was divided up between the Mayor and Senator Matheussen." Talk about being delusional! Lanholm was totally out of line for repeating such a state-

ment without any proof, the Judiciary Committee was wrong in accepting the testimony of Lanholm's recollection of a third-party conversation without corroboration, and Mrs. Weber did not know what she was talking about!

12. Predicated upon the letter written by Superior Officers Burke, Dumont, Lanholm, Condit and Zbikowski's, dated July 29, 1999 and addressed in the following fashion by the Gloucester County Times, might we conclude that their real problem was with the Mayor's heritage, not his performance.

SATURDAY, AUGUST 7, 1999 – TIMES EDITORIAL

Jeers to the Washington Township police officers who attacked Mayor Gerald Luongo in a letter to the media, and used a vile ethnic slur against Italians in a feeble attempt to build their case. We won't repeat their idiotic remark here, but the next letter the two lieutenants and two captains write should be one of resignation since they can't serve the Italian community because they evidently hold these hard-working citizens in such contempt. Better yet, the township should make them an offer they can't refuse: Quit or be fired.

The simple reason why the Democratic members of Council would not take this advice and subsequent action is obvious: the superior officers were doing what they were told to do by Council. The promise of no reprisals for their actions, the promise of the Chief's job in due time, the knowledge that once the superior officers had reclaimed their power, nothing could stop them in pursuing those officers they believed to be supportive of the Mayor, and finally, the payback to Boss Sweeney in naming "one of their own" as the Director of the Gloucester County Police Academy. This was the superior officers' 30 pieces of silver.

THE ULTIMATE BETRAYAL

Another tempest in a teapot orchestrated by Council and apparently implemented by one of their minions for whatever reason, was the recording of a meeting that I had in my office with three people whom I trusted. In June of 1999, I met with Chief Sowney, Deputy Chief Murphy and Jacquie Lauletta, Director of Personnel. The meeting was simply an opportunity for me to vent a great deal of frustration that had been building up with regard to Council's constant meddling into everything, including the Letter of No Confidence against the Chief and the apparent division of the department into two factions, as noted by Lloyd Dumont in his memo to a subordinate officer. I also voiced anger about certain officers who seemed to be in the midst of all the problems and their unabashed political machinations on Township time. There were pockets in the community where seemingly nothing would satisfy certain residents, which I found particularly difficult, as I prided myself on solving problems, not creating them. All this, coupled with the press who was unrelenting and, in my opinion, unfairly attacking the Affordable Housing Plan regardless of the facts, made for a very difficult and stressful winter and spring with no letup in sight. I was like any other elected leaders who are concerned how much politics is grabbing hold of a government that had taken pride in keeping politics outside where it belonged. That was the extent of the meeting. Names were mentioned and unkind things said in the heat of the moment, but nothing to garner the attention that the tape elicited. (And on the subject of the harsh comments that I made about certain employees, I personally apologized to them and never denied nor attempted an excuse. Time would prove me correct—these people were not as magnanimous as I. But then again, that is their karma!)

I would venture to say that I was probably the only person who ever paid any attention to Jim Murphy. Over the years he was regarded by his colleagues as a fixture in the police department. He did his job, socialized very little and I doubt that anyone really knew anything about his personal life, a life that I came to find out was absent of friends and meaningful interpersonal relationships. However, I saw in Murphy an intelligent resource that had been overlooked by many of his superiors simply because he kept to himself and rarely got involved with any ancillary and frivolous aspects of the police department. In brief, he did his job! For that reason, I promoted him to Deputy Chief since I knew that he and Sowney would be the "dream team" to lead the men and women of the department into an area of community policing. I gave Murphy my friendship, my loyalty, my trust and my word. I never once doubted anything Jim Murphy did and relied on him to support Wil Sowney 100 percent.

The events that began in mid-July of 1999, while I was on our annual family vacation in North Carolina, will to this day be a mystery and a source of disbelief and disappointment. I received a call from a friend who told me that a tape recording had been released of a private meeting that was held in my office. I racked my brain but for the life of me, I knew of no meeting that would have any reason to be taped, or worse, released to the public. Of course, with the Judiciary Committee, whose operations were suspect, and given the past record of political harassment heaped on me by Lyons, Rapposelli and Davidson, anything was possible. These people and their allies were treacherous! As had been the case for every family vacation since becoming Mayor, there was something amiss in the Township and I was to have no rest.

When I was told that it was a tape that Murphy had made in June at a meeting that included me, the Chief and Mrs. Lauletta, I said, "Absolutely not." Knowing that Murphy would never hurt me, I called his pager number and within a few minutes, I received a call back. Murphy wanted to know who was calling since he didn't recognize the North Carolina exchange. I told him, "It's the Mayor, Jim, how are you?" He immediately responded, "I can't talk to you and you will need to contact my attorney." I knew then that the man I trusted implicitly and unconditionally was another Judas. I called my office and requested that "the tape" be sent to me. It arrived by FedEx the next day and I listened to the entire tape. Frankly, it was much ado about nothing. So I was angry and so I said some unkind things about people that were perhaps harsh and inappropriate. I was saying them to people I trusted, in my private office, and whose confidences I never violated when they spoke about individuals—most notably, members of the police department. I knew that this was just another diversion created by the Democrats. Of more concern was the fact that Murphy came to that meeting and surreptitiously recorded not only the Mayor, but his alleged friend, colleague and boss. Why would anyone do this? What kind of person would stoop so low? What were Jim Murphy's motives?

Well, I will never know the answers to those questions and frankly it doesn't matter. Murphy disappeared for the next eight weeks or so, which prompted me to write him and ask if he was abandoning his position. The consensus among the members of the police department was that he was afraid to face anyone since his credibility was reduced to zero. His response to me was directed through his lawyer, which was unusual but it indicated that he was attending conferences and taking vacations, all without any paperwork being filed in the normal course of personnel policy.

Finally, Murphy put his reasons for his actions into writing to Carl Postiglione, PBA President and Edmund Giordano, FOP President. Murphy indicated that he recorded the meeting because he thought his job to be in jeopardy as a result of the events taking place in the police department. I found that comment very interesting. I had never indicated to him in any of the many meetings that he and Sowney had with me in the weeks prior to that June meeting, anything other than my trust, unconditional support and unequivocal belief that BOTH of them were working hard and doing a great job in keeping the department operational in spite of Burke,

Dumont and the other less vocal superior officers. Therefore, if Murphy's job was not the issue at that June meeting, why did he keep a tape and make a copy? Was he planning to blackmail me, thinking that I would say something that was a revelation and perhaps incriminating? He never explained how Lyons knew he had a tape, why Lyons requested the tape and why he (Murphy) brought the tape to the Judiciary Committee hearing. Murphy stated that he was under oath and required to tell the truth. The question, Mr. Murphy: What is the truth? Taping your superior at a private meeting and giving it to people who you know are his adversaries—is that TRUTH? Did Matthew Lyons order you to make a tape in the hopes that I would state something incriminating? What did Lyons think that I would say? I never did one illegal act while serving as Mayor and that is a matter of fact, not personal opinion. Were you promised something from Council for your complicity? What did I ever do to hurt you? Did you support Wil Sowney, the man you called friend, or were you undermining him, taking orders from Burke and Dumont in doing whatever was necessary to get Sowney to quit? And finally, how did the tape get released to the public, when allegedly the tape was offered as evidence in a PRIVATE AND CONFIDENTIAL HEARING? What kind of person would be so absent of conscience as to go out of his way to hurt another person?

TALKING ABOUT CHARACTER

Both Jim Murphy and Robert Burke (former Chief's Burke's brother) were sued by a young woman who worked as a dispatcher for the Township for sexual harassment. For all the complaints that former Chief Burke would make about fellow officers, his silence about his brother's activities was deafening.

Many officers and I testified in depositions against Murphy and Burke. I had the unpleasant task of listening to the rather disgusting taped phone calls from both Murphy and Burke to this young woman. I also sat with this young woman for hours and listened to her story how working as a dispatcher for the Township was difficult under these circumstances but she needed a job to support herself and a small child. Written testimony from fellow female dispatchers and female officers established a pattern of sexual harassment by Deputy Chief Murphy and civilian employee Robert Burke. I wondered how these men could have so much time on their hands as to bother this woman or to even think that what they were doing was appropriate. I think that the public would agree that this kind of behavior is pathetic and unconscionable.

When the superior officers demonstrated their disrespect for their superiors, which was in direct violation of the Policy and Procedures and went undisciplined due to Council's interference, a breakdown in the chain of command within the rank and file developed. And as if there wasn't enough nonsense, I found myself dealing with yet another problem: numerous calls from the police department to a 900 area code (verified to be sexually explicit). Although it was impossible to determine who was making these calls, it was obvious that certain officers *really* had too much time on their hands.

This young woman used good judgment, as did her lawyer, once they realized that the Township didn't have a leg to stand on with regard to the behavior of Murphy and Burke. What has become a hallmark and seemingly routine action of the Davidson Administration, a settlement was reached and the taxpayers paid for the mistakes of Council. Burke and Murphy should have been fired! Of course, thanks to the settlement, Murphy and Burke were spared the embarrassment and humiliation of a trial. Now that Fran Burke was Police Chief, his brother was protected; Murphy was being protected by Council as a reward for his collusion in the Judiciary Committee's hearings. No one was fired. An undisclosed settlement was paid and the young woman transferred to the County Dispatch Center and got on with her life.

Although the superior officers, especially Burke and Dumont, attempted to blame everything that was wrong in the police department on my alleged interference, the truth be told, their lack of performing the duties for which they were being handsomely paid was really at the core of the problem. The Superior Officers were playing politics and dancing to the tune played by pipers Lyons, Rapposelli, Davidson and Sweeney. Certain people had personal agendas and they were going to be played out regardless of the cost.

COUNCIL SHOWS POLITICAL VENGEANCE

Chief Sowney retired by the end of 1999, against my wishes. I knew that his handpicked leadership team had done him dirt by running him out and, frankly, I wanted him to stand tall and fight back. He was particularly disappointed with Murphy, whom he had trusted. His resignation was accepted with little or no reaction from Council.

Once again, I embarked upon a search for a Police Chief and once again, I opened the door to Council to be part of the process. If Murphy had been the stand-up guy that I believed he was before he decided to make me the enemy, he would have been the next Chief of Police. Murphy had mentioned in the letter to the union presidents that he did what he did "upon advice." I think that perhaps his "advice" was coming from an "advisor" who had a personal agenda. Although I could not trust Lyons, Rapposelli or Davidson, I nevertheless extended an olive branch. When the interviews were over, Lyons presented me with a list of superior officers and indicated that Council would be supportive of any one of the individuals for Chief. I decided the best choice, the most knowledgeable person, a man who would not be intimidated or bought off with promises of personal gain was the Fraternal Order of Police President, Edmund Giordano. I had once been very critical of Giordano until I personally reviewed his personnel file. He was not liked by his superiors because they couldn't control and manipulate him. He stood tall and was not afraid to stand alone. Giordano's failure to become a superior officer was simply due to jealousy. It was never too late to rectify a wrong, so I appointed him Chief of Police. Council voted along party lines and voted against him, which didn't mean a thing other than to show their true colors of anger and revenge. Council's plan to put their puppet in the Chief's seat was foiled. Although Council challenged my authority to take this action, the Superior Court upheld my right to do what I did and pretty much told Council to take a hike.

Chief Giordano did an outstanding job for this community. For those officers who took the time to take a good objective look at what he was doing for the department, and who had the courage of their own convictions, stood up and admitted that Giordano was an exceptional leader. But true to Lloyd Dumont's self-fulfilling prophecy, the department remained somewhat divided with the anti-Giordano team going underground, working by cover of darkness and by subterfuge against him and those they considered supportive of him.

In spite of these internal problems and the open defiance and disrespect of the Democrats on Council in refusing to recognize him as Chief of Police, Edmund Giordano joined Fred Reeves, Richard Moore and Wil Sowney as one of Washington Township's best leaders. (My prediction is that Charles Billingham appointed May 1, 2004 as Chief of Police will join the above leaders.)

REMEMBERING IS GOOD FOR THE SOUL

I have always been loyal to a fault. Respect that we give to people who have helped us in our lives does not require the person to pay homage or to constantly demonstrate outward signs of loyalty. I liken this to one's belief in religion. You don't need to go around telling and showing everyone that you believe in God or that you are a good person because you have done this and that! People can tell what you are like by watching and observing you through your deeds and by your actions. This silent respect or appreciation also manifests itself when others around you may denigrate a person you know. Those people many times do not have a clue to what this person is really like. You would walk away from such a conversation or quietly say, "You don't know what you are talking about," but at least you wouldn't become a party to the conversation because you lack the courage to stand up and to be counted. No one is asking anyone to put their life on the line for them or to do any extraordinary deed. Sure, many people have and that is deeply appreciated but never expected or requested.

In a small community like Washington Township, people are hired for jobs because they are recommended for employment by people who know the person in charge. All things being equal in terms of ability and credentials, employers tend to rely on recommendations as a vital factor in the hiring process. This process works amazingly well and is far from an anomaly. What causes the problem in what could be a professional relationship predicated on a mutual respect is when the employee decides that he/she was the ONLY person qualified for the position and that he/she would have been hired regardless of what anyone did for him/her. When that kind of thinking begins to control the way the recipient treats the person who provided the opportunity that may have otherwise been denied, that lack of gratitude hurts the donor and makes him wonder if he did the right thing.

I have had my share of employees turn their backs on me for whatever reason. When they needed a job or were looking for a promotion, they sought me out. When their proverbial butts were being kicked by a superior—in some cases, out the door—they had no problem finding me. When all I needed was their moral support, they were nowhere to be found. I cannot respect silence as an acceptable manner in which to address a grievance or displeasure with a person. When people are afraid to face another and to speak their minds usually they are hiding something, lying or involved in a treacherous situation that will speak to their lack of character and integrity. People like this are eventually exposed and lose the esteem regardless of their position, of those forced to work with or for them!

Council tried to imply by use of unreliable testimony from a third party that police officers paid to get their jobs. I know that is a lie. In all my years in politics I never personally approached any employee to even purchase a ticket or to donate to a campaign fundraiser on my behalf. I prided myself on the ability to keep politics out of the work place. I challenge anyone who says he paid to get a job in this community to contact the Attorney General of this State and to provide him with the details so that he can take appropriate action. There will be no anonymity, as with Council's Judiciary Committee that entertained baseless allegations, hearsay, gossip and outright lying. Rather, the complainant will need to give the proof that substantiates the charge. It is a serious charge, but if you believe it to be true, then it must be addressed!

The vast majority of police officers hired on my watch were residents of the community. My position on hiring employees was that residents as equally qualified as non-residents were given preference. Regardless of the Mayor's recommendation to the Chief of Police for the hiring of a police officer, there was a process and procedure conducted by the department to ensure that candidates were qualified either to be hired directly due to certification or to attend the Academy for training. Each year several hundred letters and/or applications for the police department were received. Without the Mayor's recommendation, many individuals would be just another application placed in the files. I didn't create the process and from all reports, the process is the same in many other towns. For those officers who have chosen to forget how they got their jobs, all I ask of you is to be honest with yourself. You too may have benefited from one or more of the following "other factors" that ensured that you were hired:

- I personally knew you as you were growing up and when you approached me about a job, I did what I could for you.

- Your parents knew me personally and spoke to me on your behalf.

- You had the recommendation of a friend, a religious leader, a teacher or a counselor who had my ear.

- You had a relative in the police department who came to me and spoke on your behalf.

- You were recommended to me from a member of Council or from an elected official from another community.

- You were a member of the Township's Police Explorers Program and your service record was impeccable.

- You had a parent who worked for the Township.

You had a "home court" advantage over equally qualified people because of one or more of these reasons and there is nothing wrong with that. The business of government is political in many ways and we all need to be reminded sometimes who offered us the hand of friendship when we needed it most. I budgeted ample funding for the department and negotiated contracts in a timely and equitable fashion. No matter what the issue or the grievance, I listened to all sides and made a decision predicated on the facts. Many of you were there through the good times and the bad. You never once turned your back on me, took pride in knowing me and even placed yourself in harm's way in the name of loyalty. You truly understand the meaning of commitment, respect and loyalty. For those who fit this definition, you know who you are and I thank you for being there.

The Roll Call 1989 - 2000

Attanasi, Tim	Billingham, Charles
Breen, Timothy	Calvello, Marty
Chalow, Jennifer	Coccia, Joseph
Conti, Michael	Crovetti, Rayne
Cushane, Thomas	Dean, Jeffrey
DiBuonaventura, J.	DiTullio, Tom
Egizi, Gary	Fisler, Matthew

Frattali, Lisa
Greer, Joseph
Gurcsik, Pat
Hilbert, George
Kennedy, Ken
LaMonica, V.
Leonard, Richard
Lombardo, John
Micucci, Joseph
Muniz, Raphael
Pelosi, Christopher
Postiglione, Lori
Ruh, Robert
Sims, Dennis
Stokley, Robert
Vena, Joseph

Gaidosh, Robert
Gurcsik, Frank
Haley, T.
Jackson, Brandy
Kurz, Michael
Lee, William
Leone, Anthony
Martin, Paul
Moore, Danny
Navan, Steven
Postiglione, Carl
Rolando, Steven
Russo III, Joseph
Spataro, Dante
Townsend, Wm.
Wisley, Charles

MAJOR PROMOTIONS 1989-2000

Lt. Steve Augello
Lt. Ken Condit
Lt. Lloyd Dumont
Deputy Chief James Murphy

Cpt. Francis Burke
Lt. J. Dalessandro
Cpt. J. Gallagher
Lt. Fran Vannoni

OTHER PROMOTIONS 1989-2000

Cpl. Tim Attanasi
Sgt. Charles Billingham*
Cpt. Steve Branco
Inv. Joseph Coccia
Sgt. Eric Conova
Sgt. William Flaherty
Cpl. Joseph Greer
Sgt. Joseph Hollingsworth
Cpl. Vincent Lamonica
Sgt. Darin Lloyd
Inv. Arthur Michelson
DSG. Bernie Rodgers
Cpl. Joseph Russo

Lt. John Bates
Cpl. R. Borkowski
Det. Louis Brecht
Cpl. Jim Connor
Inv. Matthew Fisler
DSG. A. Garczynski
Cpl. Pat Gurcsik
Cpl. Ken Kennedy
Det. Richard Leonard
Sgt. D. MacKenzie
DSG. Rafael Muniz
Det. Steve Rolando
Inv. Patricia Sherry

Det. Richard Sumek   Sgt. John Szigethy
Cpl. William Townsend   Cpl. James Welding
Cpl. Robert West   Inv. Charles Wisely

(*Appointed Chief May 1, 2004) (DSG=Detective Second Grade)

CUMULATIVE EDUCATIONAL RECORDS (AS OF 2000)

60+ credits no degree	A.A degree	B.A./B.S. degree
13	31	24

M.A.or M.S. degree	M.A. +30	Total Files
07	04	79

(Source: Mayor's Exhibit/Personnel files)

FINAL THOUGHTS

The attitude of the Administration towards the police unions can be summed up in a public statement issued by the Township's present Solicitor Michael Albano: "The actions taken by the PBA and FOP against the Township are frivolous." Based on that statement one might ask, "Why, then, does the Township keep on losing?" Could the judges, arbitrators and PERC professionals ALL be wrong? Or perhaps you are correct, Mr. Albano, that there is a frivolous component to these issues and that is the intractability and lack of objectivity by former Chief Burke, his subordinates, Mayor Davidson, Jean DeGennaro Business Administrator, Councilman Matthew Lyons, and you! This analysis makes much more sense! You are the frivolous ones! (Courtesy former Police Chief Edmund Giordano.)

"In the end we will remember not the words of our enemies, but the silence of our friends."

—Martin Luther King

Chapter 25

ON THE SUBJECT OF...

T his section is a potpourri of ideas that didn't quite find their way into specific chapters in the book for many reasons. Let's call this "thinking out loud" and/ or musing on a topic.

COLLEAGUES

A personal thank you to the many fine men and women whom I have had the pleasure of meeting and serving with as a member of the New Jersey Conference of Mayors and the Gloucester County Mayors' Association. These two organizations have done much to advance the professional leadership of all elected officials.

Loyal Supporters

A debt of gratitude and appreciation to former students, friends, colleagues, constituents and other politicians for your outpouring of respect, loyalty, admiration and respect as shown by the number of letters written on my behalf. It's so nice to realize the impact you have had on people and how they regard you while you can appreciate it.

Press

"Matters of tone and motive loom large in investigative stories where writers sometimes resort to HINTS and INNU-ENDOES and SUGGESTIVE ARRANGEMENTS of damaging detail to establish what the evidence fails to demonstrate. The tone of these articles is editorial, snide and, in essence, prosecutorial. If there were solid facts to draw upon, the reader will draw his/her own conclusions without the aid of reporter's zingers. Papers go astray in trying to do alleged investigative reporting. Reporters begin to see themselves as cops rather than gathers of information. Society will get along quite well without newsrooms that view themselves as police forces."

—Gene Roberts, retired Executive Editor, Philadelphia Inquirer

People

I understand the NIMBY people (Not In My Back Yard) and the CAVE people (Citizens Against Virtually Everything). I respect your right to disagree with decisions made by those elected to serve you. I also respect your right to attend meetings and to express your opinions. What I never understood is why so many people believe that because an elected official may support a project that the people object to, why do you believe that said politician is a crook or is in someone's pocket? Don't elected officials have the right to an opinion based upon their research? Does the public always think that they are right because they are in the majority?

When the public complains about property tax increases, do they forget that the members of the municipal government, the Board of Education and the Fire District and other taxing entities who have developed these budgets also live in the community and they too must pay the very same taxes?

Why do so few people take an interest in voting on school budgets? Do you know that most school board elections only attract about 10%-19% of the registered voters in most communities? Do you know that the average school budget represents 65%-75% of your property tax dollars?

Everyone complains about the traffic, yet so few use the bus routes established by public transportation. The people of Gloucester County lobbied the County Freeholders to vote NO on billions of dollars in federal aid to establish a passenger light-rail system on preexisting rail beds. Given the number of traffic signals installed along the various roadways in our area providing access to major roadways and controlled intersections, how come people still complain?

There are always complaints about speeders in local neighborhoods. When police patrols were told to issue a summons with NO warnings, how come we always caught the local neighbors speeding and not the "strangers" as reported?

I never believed in speed humps on public roads. They are more of a danger than a deterrent to speeding.

Why is it that when people attend a Council meeting they always seem to forget, or worse, deny the efforts of the Mayor and his staff in attempting to resolve your problem? Not all problems can be resolved to everyone's satisfaction.

Does anyone ever attend County government meetings?

Does it surprise the public to know that regardless of whether an elected official is a Republican, Democrat or Independent, there are few elected officials who are committed and dedicated to the people and would do anything it takes to resolve your problem or concern?

Why does the public feel that it is okay to shout, yell and at times, even hurl obscenities at elected officials at public meetings? Considering that these elected officials also live in the community, aren't they entitled to a degree of civility? What message does this send to our youth? Is this the kind of message that we should be sending to our kids through our public behavior?

Does the public really believe that it is okay to cheer for a member of the public who supports their position but perfectly all right to shout down another member of the public who disagrees with the majority?

If a resident purchases a home without finding out the zoning of vacant land in the area or who chooses to ignore signs indicating the proposed use of vacant land, why do residents think that they have the right to lobby government to change that zoning in order to benefit themselves while denying the landowner his rights?

Why does the public object to the methods a politician must employ in fund raising? How else do you raise money to get elected or to fend off adversarial attacks? Can you name even ONE politician who got elected without advertising in print, on the radio or on television?

POLITICS AND POLITICIANS

I always wondered what I did to William Bailey, a professor at Gloucester County College, to elicit so much criticism in his Letters to the Editor about me. Time has told the tale:

1. Bailey is close friends with former WT police officer Lloyd Dumont, who has publicly and unabashedly demonstrated his disdain and prejudice against me as an Italian-American. Bailey was Dumont's campaign manager for an exploratory campaign for County Sheriff.

2. Bailey and his co-instructor, Professor Dave Roberts, were appointed to the Police Academy Advisory Board. This broke years of cooperation between the Gloucester County Freeholders and the Gloucester County Police Chief's Association. In the past, the GCPCA would make recommendations to the County Freeholders for appointed members to the Police Academy's Advisory Board.

3. In 1999-2000, the year of the Bailey and Roberts appointments, Chief Pat Kuchinsky (Glassboro) and Chief Ken Ridinger (Paulsboro) were recommended by the

GCPCA to the Advisory Board. The Gloucester County Freeholders, under Sweeney's direction and without explanation, denied the recommendation. In addition to the unprecedented action of appointing Bailey and Roberts, Sweeney appointed Chief Jim Mahaffey (West Deptford). Mayor Dave Shields was Mahaffey's boss and the boss of the Gloucester County Improvement Authority as well as a very close political ally of Sweeney.

4. The Gloucester County Police Chief's Association wrote a letter of protest to the Gloucester County Freeholders objecting to this unprecedented action, which was a slap in the face to the membership of the GCPCA. The objection fell on deaf ears and Sweeney summarily dismissed the Police Chief's objection to this obviously political move with the support of Freeholder Bob Smith, a Sweeney puppet and political yes man.

5. Having the votes needed for his appointment, Lloyd Dumont was made Director of the Gloucester County Police Academy. This was his reward for dropping out of the Sheriff's race and for creating rancor in the Township's Police Department. Dumont was not the most qualified for the position, but in politics, qualifications are unimportant, as so vividly demonstrated in this specific situation.

6. Dumont was also directed by Sweeney to launch an all-out attack on me, doing whatever it took to get me out of office. Dumont was also helped by Freeholder Bob Smith in return for Dumont's help in Smith's bid for the As-

sembly. Sweeney also directed another minion, Kenny Gwertz, County Director of Public Works to attend Township Council meetings and create discord, something that Gwertz did so very well. The plan that Sweeney orchestrated worked quite well.

7. As a final act to register displeasure with what the Freeholders had done and disappointment with the degree of political corruption that had infected the Police Academy Advisory Board, only ONE police chief from the Association attended Dumont's retirement dinner. This act of reasonable and understandable defiance by the Gloucester County Police Chiefs Association demonstrated their integrity and refusal to be manipulated by Boss Sweeney. Of course, Fran Burke of the Washington Township Police Department wrote a nasty letter to the Chiefs Association, chastising members for their actions and supporting his crony and partner in subterfuge and character assassinations, Dumont. After all, Burke's reward was also contingent on my political demise and he too followed his marching orders from Sweeney. Sweeney, the master puppeteer, had no shortage of puppets.

Why do people like Lloyd Dumont act out as they do? Is the need for power so great as to corrupt one's character? Are we expected to accept any kind of behavior in the name of politics? In 1990 when the late Richard Moore came to me and requested that I appoint Dumont to the police force, I had reservations. He left the force in 1976 and joined the

Gloucester County Prosecutor's Office, only to resign circa 1985 for punching a superior officer in what appeared to be an alcohol-related incident in a local bar. He bounced around for a while and in 1990-91 wanted to come home. Rather than start at the bottom and work his way up, he was immediately assigned to and formed the DARE unit. During my tenure as Mayor, I promoted him three times.

I also respected him for his work and commitment to the Jewish Defense League, which brought him due recognition. When Dumont began to attack me in 1999 with this Mafia nonsense, the godfather/don characterizations and other remarks that denigrated all Italian-Americans, I was shocked. His lame excuse of being a professor of Italian Crime Studies didn't cut it with me and the public, since crime and the Mafia had nothing to do with my family lineage or, in fact, with the majority of Italians. But this type of political prejudice can work if properly used through what is called "black public relations." Dumont got the ball rolling. He was retiring from the Township Police Force and had a job guarantee. The mindless superior officers of the Township under Burke's leadership put their Italian ethnic slurs and attacks into writing in an attempt to justify their character assassination against me. This disgusting display of prejudice justifiably warranted them an Editorial in the *Gloucester County Times* that said that they should all be fired! However, as noted before, Lyons, Rapposelli and Davidson had promised Burke the Chief's job and the superior officers were being protected because of their testimony before the Judicial Committee. It was also rumored that if Davidson were to be elected Mayor,

Rapposelli would resign Council and be appointed solicitor for the MUA or possibly the Planning Board (this explains Rapposelli's failure to respond to the ethnic slurs considering that he too is Italian.) This was another well orchestrated plan that benefited Dumont and Burke, but did nothing for the superior officers. These superior officers are viewed with disdain by their fellow officers, regarded as bigots by the public and are in serious need of sensitivity training. I doubt that any of them will advance any further unless they once again permit themselves to be used as political prostitutes. It appears that many have opted for retirement and that is good for the Community and the police department.

With regard to the superior officers and Chief Francis Burke, I often wonder how you justify the hurt that you inflicted upon a few of Washington Township's finest simply because you associated them as friends of mine. These men had some great ideas that did much to improve the department and you demeaned those ideas and the officers. You crossed over the line of common decency just to get even and that, no matter how you cut it, is sick. Do you realize that all the emotional pain that you inflicted on others will come back to haunt you one day? You cannot do what you have done to others and expect that you will not be called to answer.

POLITICIANS USE THE PRESS

Another willing ally in what I have determined was a carefully orchestrated smear campaign against me was Maureen Graham, a reporter for the *Philadelphia Inquirer* who was always looking for corruption and the Mafia around every corner. She is one of those people who always see the negative in everything and is quite crafty at getting members of the public to willingly enter her web of deception. From the time that she was thrown out of my first campaign office in 1988, she has always found something negative to write about me or my political supporters. In fact, the first story that I recall that Graham wrote after I took office in 1989 was a negative one. The story refers to my very close friends who worked on my campaign as members of a *junta*. (A junta is a small group of people ruling a country after a coup d'etat.) The term is a pejorative one. The photo that accompanied the story was taken of the home owned by the Laulettas, my longtime friends. This was not just a photo of a home that one would see in a real estate advertisement, but rather, the photo was taken through a group of trees on an acute angle so as to make the home look ominous.

Graham was also crafty when it came to taking quotes out of context, placing them in a paragraph that would then adulterate them into something foreign to the actual statement that the individual made in good faith. One of my idle pastimes was comparing Graham's stories to other reporters' stories and wondering if Graham was at the same meeting or at the meeting at all. Another annoying aspect of Ms. Graham's need to "write her story" was her insidious referring to friendships as though they were evil. She also repeated things from the past as though they just happened yesterday. This repetition was carefully woven into the majority of her stories therefore giving the *perception* that something was wrong when, in fact, there was nothing amiss.

When it came to Lloyd Dumont and the superior officers' unrelenting attacks on me through the anti-Italian hate
letters and statements, Graham was very resourceful in finding several Italian-Americans in the community who didn't
take umbrage with the use of Mafia, godfather, don, etc. These
few residents were happy to disclose that they were *close
friends of Mob figures* and the terms that the Mayor was up-
set about were part of Italian history. It is a sad day for those
individuals when they believe that their heritage is defined
by *The Untouchables, The Godfather* and *The Sopranos.* That
so-called history focused on a secret society of gang members involved in criminal activity and has nothing to do with
the centuries of Italian history or the legions of chronicles
that depict the numerous contributions that Italians have
made to all of civilization. The terms used by Burke, Dumont,
the superior officers, Bob Smith and others regardless how
you try to euphemize them, are negative and offensive and
considered inappropriate. It seemed that all the anti-defa-
mation organizations agreed with my position.

When Graham took on the writing of *her perception* of
the Affordable Housing Plan as seen through the eyes of the
Democratic party whose agenda was so obvious, she did a
disservice to the community, demeaned the hard work of
many individuals (including Judge Francis), and gratuitously
made a wasteland of my life in the process. Graham's ability
to casually interface with either the Philadelphia or Cherry
Hill Office of the F.B.I. should give pause to all Americans
about the confidentiality of this government agency.

Setting aside the rhetoric of the Democratic Party and Graham's insipid stories, let's look at the facts that were blatantly obvious, reported to the press but for the purpose of a story, but never printed. The statements listed below are absolutely true and have not been disputed by any legitimate governmental agency.

1. There was no impropriety or illegality with any actions relative to the Affordable Housing Plan or any one of its many components.

2. I was never once interviewed or questioned by the F.B.I. during the entire period that the Affordable Housing Plan became an issue which was ALL of 1999 and 2000.

3. The Affordable Housing Plan and all its components were resolved and approved two years earlier and all records were public and available both locally and at the State Offices of COAH.

4. No files were removed from the Municipal Building with regard to this matter by the F.B.I. By law all files were public record.

5. No computers were seized by the F.B.I. nor removed from the Municipal Building contrary to the statements made by then Chief Francis Burke in the early part of 2001.

This whole flap over the Affordable Housing Plan was a result of Raymond Rapposelli calling the F.B.I. in December of 1998. He informed them that he had been approached by his business partner Anthony Marotta, who was soliciting

$2500 from each of the 12 or 13 local businessmen and professionals who were investors in the corporation that held title to the County House Road site. This was prior to the Ingerman Group purchasing the site for one of the Affordable Housing Projects and the Township's subsequent purchase of a parcel of that land from Ingerman for the Soccer Complex. The events, as I now understand them to be, are that when the F.B.I. questioned Marotta, he denied that he ever said any such thing. Subsequently, the other investors gave statements to the F.B.I. denouncing Rapposelli's statements and dismissing the allegation as politically motivated. There was *no* corroboration of Rapposelli's statement and yet, from that point forward, the F.B.I. invested over two years of taxpayers' money in attempting to prove that I took a bribe in this project.

The allegation by Rapposelli was an outright lie, which was permitted to fester because the F.B.I. refused to bring closure to this matter in an expedient fashion. The agency permitted this character assassination to escalate by refusing to act in a timely fashion, leading the people to believe that the F.B.I. was proceeding vigorously and successfully with an investigation. In fact, a document in the possession of the F.B.I. thought to be a key component in this alleged bribery case was found to be a forgery! To this day I have yet to find out who gave this forged document to the F.B.I. and I ask, "Why hasn't this person been prosecuted?"

Anyone who followed the process from beginning to end would come to the same conclusion. In fact, Rapposelli, who started this calculated smear campaign, was so cavalier when he said that he would give up his $25,000 profit on the investment if found out that the process in selling the land was anything other than legal. Of course he was confident in making that statement because he knew that his allegation was a lie and that he would never be required to put his money where his big mouth was! Actions do indeed speak louder than words! In the case of the F.B.I., their patent statement "We cannot either deny or confirm" leads the public to draw their own conclusions about a person or situation and that conclusion is usually a negative one. My life was destroyed by arrogant reporters and government bureaucrats who peddled groundless innuendo, half-truths and false information.

POLITICIANS AND PLUNDER

Many politicians are especially adept at using people and the press for their personal agenda. One such politician is former Freeholder and present Assemblyman Robert "Bob" Smith. I believe that Smith has been at the public trough all his adult life. I first met Smith when he ran on my ticket in the early 1990's for Council, along with Sam Hart. Smith wasn't much of a team player. I perceived him to be pompous, arrogant and conceited. He enjoyed the financial security of my ability to fund raise, but he had his own style of campaigning that was inconsistent with the philosophy to which Sam Hart and I subscribed. With the assistance of his very close friend, fellow-worker, and political confidant Dave Fanslau, they ran a sub-campaign of personal attacks against

John Rogale, who Smith perceived as his nemesis. Smith lost the election, blaming me for his defeat when in fact he was his own worst enemy.

He continued to work for the County while attending law school, which was a beautiful arrangement for him. In the next election, Smith decided to run for Council and buck the party-endorsed slate. Of course, he was willing to withdraw his candidacy in exchange for a political job, which was provided. I would venture to say that his income from political appointments and political positions outweighs any income he makes in private practice. Smith is thoroughly a political animal that knows all too well how to use the system and people.

Smith was one politician who never ran a campaign on the issues. His style was steeped in personal attacks and distortions of the truth in order to get elected. During the Assembly campaign of 1999, Smith tried to smear me when he released a story to the *Gloucester County Times* that a recreational site that the Township had purchased was contaminated. His information was wrong! To the delight of many people, Smith was exposed as a liar. In the Assembly race of 1999, Smith avoided every issue and simply hammered me with the distortions provided by Maureen Graham, amplified the ethnic attacks of Lloyd Dumont, and denigrated my friends, Frank and Jacqui Lauletta. My work in the legislature that garnered me the Press Corps Freshman Legislator of the Year recognition, having had 37 of my bills signed into law, my work on the H.O.P.E. scholarship program and my outstanding constituent services, were totally obscured by the most negative campaign ever waged against me in print and through the media. It was in a word, disgusting!

If there was a Crocodile Tears Award or an award for Miss Disingenuous, it would go to Councilwoman Randee Davidson. In 1999, the Democrats on Council wanted to appoint a political ally, Jill Smith to a position of Deputy Clerk. I reminded Council that this job had been eliminated from the budget in previous years because it was unnecessary and a waste of the taxpayer's dollars. That didn't matter to them. Smith needed to be rewarded. Because I would not budge on this matter, Lyons, Rapposelli and Davidson threatened that they would not reappoint Mrs. Pat Lamonica, the present Township Clerk, who was a respected and much-loved longtime employee, replacing her with the politically connected Jill Smith.

The public meeting at which this was to take place was standing room only. People were outraged and spoke their mind. Finally Council decided to go into Executive Session to discuss the matter. In full view of the public, Davidson hugged and comforted Pat Lamonica as though she really cared. Talk about drama and insincerity, Davidson could take the Oscar! All Davidson had to do was to voice her objections in public, call for a vote and along with her vote and the votes of Councilmen Hart and Szczerbinski, Pat Lamonica's job was secure. Davidson was told how to vote and regardless of what was right, fair and just, Davidson would do as she was told to do.

In the closed session, Lyons made at least three phone calls to Jill Smith relative to her "salary demands" to which

Council acquiesced. Those demands required that Pat Lamonica's salary be increased in order to keep a respectable differential between the Clerk and the Deputy Clerk. Hart and Szczerbinski only agreed to vote in favor of the action to insure Pat Lamonica's reappointment. Some would call this good politics. I call it extortion and blackmail! (Jill Smith is NOT related to Robert Smith. She is now Mrs. Jill Smith-McCrea and no longer works for the Township.)

A public question for Senator Steve Sweeney: when you were Freeholder Director, why did you work so hard to find Bob Smith's close friend and political confidant David Fanslau a job after he was recorded on tape making ethnic slurs against Ted Bradley, a Black American who worked in one of the County's public offices? From all reports, the people of Logan Township absolutely did not want Fanslau as their Business Administrator and yet it seemed that the governing body was forced to hire him!

Former Council President John Maier, you really do need to watch what you say in public because words and actions have a way of coming around and biting you in your derrière. Although I knew your father and late mother very well and had a great deal of respect and admiration for them, I never had the occasion to meet you in their company. My first meeting with you was when I was campaigning with Bea Cerkez, the former Mayor of Deptford who was then running for the Freeholder Board. Along with several other candidates, we were walking your street when you arrived home from work. You accosted Cerkez in the street and unleashed a barrage of obscenities and vulgar language. You lacked control and simple civility and your behavior was obnoxious. When you ran for Council and won, do you remember your behavior when you came to my campaign headquarters to gloat? Many do! It was not a pretty sight!

When the Council and Mayor's Office failed to reach a fair and equitable agreement with the Police Union relative to their contract in 2003, you made a public statement about the police that "They stomp their feet like little children and get everything they think they deserve." You obviously were repeating what other Councilpersons have told you. This was unfortunate, since the police were responding to the violations of the law by members of the Administration who felt that they could do whatever they chose, since they had Chief Burke in their pocket. You also made another statement that contradicts the actions of Lyons, Rapposelli and Davidson: "I think that our administration has been hands-off in running the police department. For years, there was politics in the police department that should have not been there."

What you think, Mr. Maier, differs significantly from reality. The intrusion into the police department by Davidson and Lyons is part of the public record and the Courts. Former Police Chief Burke, who is a legend in his own mind, did the bidding of the Democratic politicos in causing a riff in the department, creating prejudice and disloyalty to further his own personal agenda. He sold out to the politicians no matter how hard he tries to deny it. No Mr. Maier, your perception is wrong. Had you taken the time to do your homework you would have found out for yourself just how entangled the Council on which you served had been involved with the operations of the Police Department.

POLICE, POWER AND THE PUBLIC

It is unfortunate that so many individuals elected to public office are CEO's—that's Clueless Elected Officials! If any one of them took the time to read the Township's Administrative Code or the Constitution of the United States of America, they would realize that government is able to function successfully due to a balance of power achieved through checks and balances. For any police officer to believe that he/she is above civilian review and accountability is sheer nonsense. No department or agency in government is above reproach or does it exist except to serve the best interests of the people. For a police chief to determine that any one individual in the government is too political and therefore has no place looking into or monitoring the Police Department because he/she is a civilian is without basis. In the form of government that operates Washington Township, the Mayor is empowered by law to represent the interests of the public and the well-being of all employees, regardless of their position. The Mayor's involvement into the operations of the police department or any department within the confines of the government is within his/her purview. How the employees, officers or department heads perceive that involvement is irrelevant! Charges of "political meddling" are banal and a rather lame and poor excuse for denying accountability to the public and the executive branch of government.

Gerald J. Luongo, Ph.D.

A perfect example of keeping the Police Department community-friendly and accessible was my position that Washington Township was sufficiently independent to maintain its own dispatching services. The professional men and women that operated the local Police Dispatch did a great job. In fact, I was very supportive of them when they unionized in order to give them parity with other employees. I stood firm against the County, refusing to abolish our dispatching service while replacing it with the County's system. The County had a fine system and perhaps there might be a cost savings, but not sufficient to eliminate a bastion of security for the people and visitors to our community especially on weekends, evenings and holidays when the police department would be dark except for the officers on patrol. An open door at the Police Department sends the message, "Welcome, we are here to serve and protect."

People Caught up in Political Blunders

In researching the law library at Rutgers University, I came upon a synopsis of a lawsuit that contained a rather interesting statement made by an attorney who was privy to a conversation among Township residents. The attorney felt compelled to come forth so that his testimony about the conversation was part of the record. This individual allegedly making these ethnic slurs and slanderous comments was Dina Koren, a campaign worker, campaign manager and campaign treasurer for the late Bob Berry and Ginny Weber. Koren was also Weber's Secretary and when Weber lost her re-election bid as freeholder, Koren landed a job in the County Clerk's Office at Weber's insistence. Weber, Koren and Berry were seen numerous times in the company of Maureen Graham, a reporter for the *Philadelphia Inquirer*. The following comments were made at public meetings in opposition to projects submitted by my good friend Frank Lauletta:

- "It's too bad your name's not Lauletta...you could get anything you want"

- "We're going to get those dagos."

- "I wonder who he paid off for that one."

- "That Mother F— is paying everybody off."

Koren denied making these statements. I shudder to think what may have been said behind closed doors when Berry, Weber and Koren were together and in the presence of Graham. To think that any one could hold such prejudice against Italians by referring to them as "dagos," is so hurtful. When I appointed Ed Giordano Chief of Police, superior officers were overhead making the statement, "Now we have two dagos to deal with, Giordano and Luongo."

PERSONAL PREJUDICE

It seems as though many politicians go unchallenged when making appointments to positions within government, even when they include family, friends and political allies. Unfortunately, I was never given that pass by the press or my adversaries in my appointment of Jacqui Lauletta as Personnel Director and Mayor's Aide. Her job included numerous responsibilities and she performed them all in a professional fashion. Mrs. Lauletta and her husband were lightning rods for the 12 years that I served as Mayor. I never denied my longtime friendship with the Lauletta family. I had and continue to have a deep admiration and respect for them as parents, grandparents and community-spirited individuals who display a sense of loyalty to friends.

We surround ourselves with people we trust, not with enemies. In politics, so-called friends, if tempted sufficiently to advance their personal agenda, can easily become adversaries. When you find people who are loyal to you and who will stand with you regardless of the situation, you are fortunate and you work not to lose them. The fact that Frank Lauletta was a commercial/industrial developer who invested in the community in which he lived, speaks to his desire to improve the quality of life for all residents. When a developer is willing to take the risks involved in commercial/industrial development, he deserves the respect of the community especially when he produces quality projects. When a developer returns to the community millions of dollars in revenue, he deserves our respect. When a businessman donates large sums of money to charities without personal recognition, that speaks to his generosity. Lauletta was all that! He constructed commercial/industrial complexes which produced no children and no demands on Township resources and which generated hundreds of thousands of dollars in annual taxes!

Perhaps some people were jealous of the Laulettas and simply disliked them because they were successful people.

The Laulettas worked hard for what they have and they took many risks in reaching their goals, risks that many of us would never take. They have children and grandchildren and want the same things that all of us want. I don't need to defend them or to speak on their behalf. But what was said and done to these people was wrong and without justification. Frank Lauletta *never* received any preferential treatment by any agency at the local, county or State governmental level. Because of our friendship he was held to a higher performance standard then any other developer doing work in this community.

POLITICAL NOTEBOOK

I sometimes wonder at the columns written by political reporters. I doubt any of them have ever campaigned for or served in elected office. It's one thing to write about politics and it is another to live it. I find many of their political conclusions or predictions interesting, but I must say that some of their comments about me have been rather harsh and especially unfair when I found myself in a difficult legal situation. But setting that aside, I too have a political notebook that I'd like to share with my readers:

- Will the F.B.I. ever release the details of the Christmas Tree Farm Land investigation, the impropriety of the Zoning Board and the billboard scandal that has direct ties to Mayor Davidson and even to the Governor's Office?

- What ever happened to the investigation into the $91,000 in alleged campaign contributions that was part of the billboard scandal?

- When the political reporters and analysts consider gubernatorial candidates from South Jersey, might I suggest some viable nominees to be included who would do South Jersey proud: Robert E. Andrews (D), Frank LoBiondo (R), Lou Greenwald (D), Diane Allen (R), John Adler (D).

- All the negative press about George Norcross, Jr. is not justified. He is a smart businessman who has made it to the top and once again, there are so many jealous on-lookers who would like to see him crash and burn. *It will never happen!* He is one of a handful of people involved with politics whose word is his bond and that is so re-freshing. I do believe that the press has a love affair with this guy. Did you ever think why so many people try to imitate Norcross? That's a sign of respect, which is richly deserved!

REPORTERS AND THE PRESS

The press and their respective reporters have made much more of my personal problems than necessary. As with any event involving a high-profile elected official, the press tend to sensationalize what happened. As we find so often in poli-tics, it is the *perception, not the reality* that becomes the story and, if not addressed appropriately, can become the facts.

The repetition of the story over the years makes it take on a life of its own as it is made part of subsequent political stories well after the event has taken place. The rewriting of the facts in situations like this is quite common among reporters and quite annoying. Just remember, guys, we have families and we deserve the right to be treated fairly and without prejudice!

THE POLITICAL PREDICAMENT

I will begin this saga by taking a quote from Republican Senator Alan Simpson of Wyoming: "I was toast of the town for a while. And then I was just toast. I know how this game works." As they often say, the way in which the story is told depends on who is doing the telling. Anyone who reads the newspaper or watches the news knows exactly what I am talking about.

I will have been on this earth some 66 years, approximately 50 of those years as a productive adult member of society. During my lifetime, I have never had any negative involvement with the law. I raised a loving family, cared for my children, worked hard and served my community to the best of my ability. No, I wasn't perfect! Being raised as a Roman Catholic and taught the Baltimore catechism by the nuns, I probably had sufficient conscience and guilt for a dozen or more people. I treated people fairly and throughout all my life, I trusted people unconditionally until proven otherwise. What I was about to experience was basically very foreign to me.

299

I understood that a County, State or federal prosecutor has the option of deciding whether or not a case will be prosecuted. Prosecutors have a great deal of power and use it many times as bargaining chips in soliciting more important information. That's why there are informants who often are as guilty as or even guiltier than the people that they are testifying against. The system is not perfect and the quality of the defense, the intelligence and general attitude of the jury, and the attitude of the judge are variables that can radically affect the outcome of any trial. But in the final analysis, the system, although flawed, functions successfully more times than not.

The assumption that all prosecutors are working in the best interest of the people is inaccurate. Agreed, some prosecutors are more diligent than others, but they all have egos that need to be fed. The process is politically tainted. Whether elected or appointed, prosecutor or judge, these people are involved, to some degree, in politics and the nature of their politics determines whether or not they are appointed or elected. For the lawyers who join the Department of Justice as Assistant U.S. Attorneys, it is usually their first step in their career. Depending upon their position in terms of longevity, many of them are trophy hunters looking for high-profile cases that will enable them to look good in the eyes of their superiors. Depending upon the profile of the case or the amount of time spent in the investigation, an Assistant U.S. Attorney (AUSA) is forced to prosecute a case even though under other circumstances the case would never merit any attention.

I have made those remarks to set the stage in bringing to the reader's attention the fact that I have researched several other reported incidents of politicians whose actions would parallel or to be considered more egregious than what I did and which were handled with less fanfare and resulted in an inconsequential outcome. No one in these specific cases was ever brought before a judge. No sentencing was imposed under State Election Law Enforcement Commissions, federal election laws or the federal Mandatory Sentencing Guidelines. Justice may say it is blind, but I believe that not to be the case! A prosecutor can make all the difference, and too often they are eager to make a name for themselves and therefore tend to be too anxious and often biased in determining the action that they will take in any given case. The Office of the AUSA provides press releases and is quite adept at "spinning a story."

People who tangle with the federal government in anything that involves the Internal Revenue Service or the criminal justice system need to remember that the federal government has unlimited financial resources and will wear you down by prolonging the case, destroy your credibility in the public's eye, or deplete every financial resource that you have in defending yourself. An individual involved with fighting the federal government is a perfect example of the David and Goliath story. Unfortunately, many of us don't have the accuracy of David, as proven by statistics. Statistics indicate that the Federal Justice Department wins approximately 95% of their cases. I suppose that is why 1 in every 37 Americans are felons in this country. Since 1974 the number of people who have been incarcerated ONE time has tripled. Between 2000 and 2001, there was an increase of 147,700 people or +2.3% placed into national correctional institutions. The criminal justice system is being used as a response to social problems in a way that is unprecedented. Judges are failing to recognize the life contributions of many individuals and are reluctant or incapable of understanding the remedy of Downward Departure provided to them in properly evaluating an individual on the merits of his overall contributions to society and not on the actions of one isolated incident that a prosecutor has determined to pursue. (Source: Policy and Research, Justice Policy Institute)

Throughout 1999 and 2000, I continued to do my job as Mayor and Assemblyman, though I was plagued by the continuous rhetoric against the Affordable Housing Plan and the orchestrated problems being created in the police department. In meeting after meeting, the Democratic members of Council and their cronies were unrelenting and the support from my own Republican Party was waning due to the rift that had developed between the leadership and me. Other than a few close allies, I was basically standing alone. I had come to the realization that leadership was a lonely job. Although I had read about the F.B.I. in the newspapers and their alleged investigation, I really had no concern because I knew that I had done nothing wrong. In the 24 months that followed Ray Rapposelli's call to the F.B.I. and his second call to Maureen Graham, I was never once contacted by any law enforcement agency or any person or department from the Prosecutor's Office. The ways in which I learned about the day-to-day details of the alleged investigation by the F.B.I. was from either of three sources: the newspaper, phone calls from Graham or at Council meetings from Matthew Lyons. As I look back, I made a mistake in ignoring the negative forces. I should have launched a proactive attack to defend the truth.

In February of 2001 I took the time to write a six-page letter to the F.B.I. and the Assistant U.S. Attorney assigned to this Federal District. I was very direct and I expressed my anger and displeasure with the manner in which this alleged investigation was handled. The government's lack of forthrightness made it seem to the public to be a major undercover investigation. The leaking of selective information to the press was unprofessional and was quite effective in damaging the reputation of targeted individuals. My administration prided itself on providing public access to all records and our cooperation with other agencies in the past demonstrated our willingness to cooperate. When the government implied anything to the contrary, it was doing a disservice to the people who served this community. Considering that every step of the Affordable Housing Plan was approved by numerous State agencies and the Superior Court of New Jersey, what were the government operatives thinking? How could the word of one political adversary carry so much weight? I mailed a copy of the letter to my Senators, Congressman and the White House. That's my style, but little did I realize that one does not criticize the F.B.I. or the Department of Justice! As much as I believed in the democratic process, I was about to find out how the investigatory, the prosecution and the judicial agencies can take the wind out of anyone's sails.

In my letter, I requested a meeting with the F.B.I. and the AUSA in charge of this entire matter. I was accommodated and I asked my friend who is a lawyer to accompany me. I was told verbally and in writing that the meeting was informal and was being offered as a courtesy to me. I spoke openly and candidly. At one point in the discussion it became quite evident that the AUSA had no interest in the Affordable Housing Plan at all. She had another agenda. I was brought to that meeting under a false pretense. The AUSA and the FBI had duped me. This meeting had absolutely nothing to do with Township business. When the meeting was over, I sought the services of a criminal attorney. My level of concern escalated and I knew that the ending to this story was not going to be one where everyone lived happily ever after.

The government could not find one shred of evidence to support the solitary allegation of Ray Rapposelli that I had taken a bribe in the Affordable Housing Project because it never happened. I would challenge the government to substantiate any charge of malfeasance in office since everyone knew that I was an honest, hardworking elected official and that I would never violate any fiduciary or ethical responsibility of my office. I respected the oath to which I swore to uphold.

When the prosecutors came to the realization that they had been misled by Rapposelli and were chasing their tails, they focused their inquiry as to the manner in which I handled my campaign accounts during the period of 1996 through 1999. The campaigns in question were that of the General Assembly and the Mayor. The government alleged that from some $555,000 in campaign contributions, I had used over $80,000 for personal use. I knew that to be incorrect and I planned to show the government that they were wrong. This should have been a matter for the State of New Jersey Election Law Enforcement Commission. I was prepared to submit corrected and amended reports to the Election Law Enforcement Commission and accept their decision. I was told that if I did that I would be charged with obstruction of justice. The AUSA had found a clever way to make this a federal matter by finding a federal statute under which to prosecute me.

With the cancelled checks, bank statements and some receipts, I was able to reconstruct both campaign accounts. Unfortunately many of the receipts had been disposed of when I left office and therefore, I was unable to account for $36,190.61 other than through cancelled checks and personal recollections. The application of federal guidelines to these expenditures excluded them. Considering that these monies were derived from campaign contributions, I couldn't understand what the crime was. There were politicians leasing cars, traveling with the family, paying salaries and numerous other expenditures. Why was I being held to a different standard?

I was told that the $36,190.61 should have been regarded as personal income, which was not reflected in my personal tax returns for the years in question. *I was charged with one count of Subscribing to False Income Tax Returns 26:7206 and one count of Mail Fraud 18:1341.* I agreed to rectify this matter, paying the taxes, interest and fines. Well, that wasn't good enough. The AUSA determined that I had to plead this case out, or she would seek an indictment from the Grand Jury. Efforts on my behalf by my attorney failed to change her mind. I had limited financial resources and given my legal bills for a criminal attorney, a tax attorney and the potential tax liability that I was facing, I was unable to mount a defense against the government. I made a mistake and was willing to make things right, but that apparently wasn't enough for the prosecutor. I was to be a trophy!

My lawyer advised me to take the plea from the government. To think that I was going to walk away from this after I stepped on so many toes was not going to happen. He also indicated that the AUSA had a boss who needed to see something substantial come from a two-year investigation that was estimated at a cost of at least $325,000. Think of all the press devoted to me over a two-year period. The AUSA was not about to walk away empty-handed! My family and I had enough of the Justice Department. I reluctantly signed the plea agreement and put my faith in the judicial system.

My lawyer had prepared an adequate defense, but he could have been more aggressive, especially in addressing the dramatic shenanigans of the AUSA in court. My attorney presented an excellent motion for a Downward Departure. If accepted by the judge, such a motion enables him/her to deviate from the Mandatory Sentencing Guidelines adopted in the late 1980's to ensure that all federal crimes are basically adjudicated on an equal basis. Thanks to the many people who continued to stand by me! Close to 300 people, including former students, colleagues, friends, family, and residents, wrote letters on my behalf. The report submitted by the pre-sentencing division of the court clearly spelled out that this was my first problem with the legal system and that my many years of community service and my genuine interest in people demonstrated by exceptional acts of generosity and kindness should be considered. Given a courtroom filled with supporters, the judge limited those who wanted to speak on my behalf to only four people, who did an outstanding job.

In my personal and biased opinion, the prosecutor went far beyond what was needed to be said considering my acceptance of guilt. She wanted to make sure that everyone in the courtroom heard her character assassination of me, which was delivered with a sense of vengeance. I know that I wouldn't want her job. It's a nasty one, but she seemed to like it!

The judge was most kind in highlighting all the positive contribution that I had made to education, the community and to the many people who were fortunate to be beneficiaries of my charity and kindness. I was commended for my duty to family. Nevertheless, an example needed to be set and therefore she would follow the Mandatory Sentencing Guidelines, denying the Downward Departure motion. Translated this meant that I would be sentenced to 13 months in a federal minimum-security installation. Commonly referred to as "yellow-line camp," these facilities have no cells, fences, gates or controls of that nature. President Bill Clinton remarked that any man or woman that can be restricted by a yellow line doesn't belong in prison. Of course, given the number of high-profile individuals sentenced to these camps who had privilege such as the Watergate Gang, these camps were called Club Fed.

Given time for "good behavior" I was home in 11 months and 7 days. I was also required to pay state and federal taxes on $36,190.16 income, which included interest and penalties in the amount of $29,000. The Court fined me $21,340.61, which represented the difference between the $14,850 required in restitution to those contributors requesting a refund. In the opinion of many, the penalty was double jeopardy! I paid twice for the same dollars plus I spent 11 months and 7 days in a federal prison camp. To me a financial punishment of $65,190.16 plus the 11 months and 7 days seemed a little excessive. But I am sure to some, I got off easy. Everyone is entitled to an opinion!

EPILOGUE

lthough I am not sure of the exact title, I believe a
made-for-television film, "For The Sake of Truth,"
parallels what I believe was done to me by members
of the press, political adversaries and some very misguided
people.

The film centers on the Senator Joe McCarthy era and
the famed blacklisting of TV, radio, screen, artistic performers, writers, directors and other media personalities. As you
may know, many of these professionals never worked again
and their personal lives and reputations were destroyed by a
very perverted, mean-spirited and totally misguided McCarthy
and his cronies. The film is based on an actual story and
subsequent lawsuits that made headlines in 1952. It was a
civil case and the litigant was suing for damages in the amount
of $500,000. This was a jury trial.

The performer in question was a veteran broadcaster of
CBS. He was suing a consulting firm comprised of two individuals who had established themselves as investigators who
could determine, by research and inquiry, the "real Americans" and the "Communist sympathizers." The performer
questioned CBS as to why he was fired and was never pro-

vided anything substantial. He tired quickly of the double-talk and innuendo. A close friend told him about a "list" his name appeared on with charges of "un-American activities" and other subversive acts that tied him to Communist sympathizers. This newsletter, published by the consulting firm, was mailed to all media outlets, Madison Avenue advertising firms, advertisers and sponsors of TV, radio and print. The performer soon learned that he was just one of many of his colleagues who had been blacklisted by these consultants.

Others who found themselves in this performer's situation had elected to remain silent, hoping that the situation would mitigate itself. In fact, some of these blacklisted performers paid an "investigating fee" to the consultants to re-visit their personnel file in the hopes of discovering "new information" that would clear the record. They paid the very same consultants who created the file to re-investigate it and determine any discrepancies. I believe that type of business is called blackmail or extortion.

These consultants were arrogant and pompous, regarding themselves as the guardians of truth, boastful of their intelligence and most of all, enjoyed the power that they had over people. These two men could ruin a career and/or destroy a person's good name. It was too much power for any mortal. As you are well aware, power corrupts.

These two men got into business at a time when America was looking under beds and in closets for "pinkos." And if you research the facts of that time in history, it was a politically motivated, self-serving sham by one Joe McCarthy and company. However, the timing was right! Like the people of today, the public believed that the performance industry and the media was too liberal and that all politicians have the propensity to lie, cheat and steal or at the very least, be a little dishonest. If this kind of bilge is repeated enough times, it becomes fact.

The consultants were quite creative. They established a pro-American Committee in upstate New York. The chairman was a WWII veteran and zealot. Coupled with other misguided individuals that believed in "the cause," letters were written to the press, demonstrations at public places were orchestrated and individuals appeared at public meetings and events delivering diatribes. The consultants also began to identify manufacturing companies, retail and wholesale businesses, professional firms, doctors, lawyers, teachers and others who had "known Communists working for them." Prior to a story or letter being written about any of this, the consultants would contact the owners, etc., to get a "reaction." For a modest fee, the consultants would gladly investigate the employee and, somehow or other, the story or letter that was written had a different spin on it.

As the trial evolved, it was found that all the information provided or discovered by the consultants was based on hearsay, informants, unreliable sources and unnamed officials. In fact, it was proven that there was no empirical research that even resembled an attempt at discovering the truth. There was never any incontrovertible evidence of wrongdoing. These consultants simply repeated information without verification other than to contact agencies that they knew could not, by practice, "confirm or deny." Worse yet, they strung together bits and pieces of information, out of context, leading the public to the conclusion that the person being attacked was guilty of "un-American/pro-Communist activities." Rather than deal with the wrath of an unforgiving public, employers fired employees with NO explanation. If your name made the blacklist, you were history! Today we call these methods Black PR and yellow journalism.

The story has a somewhat twisted ending. The jury realized the damage that these two reprehensible, mean-spirited and repugnant men had done to lives of good, hardworking and honest people. The jury awarded the litigant a whopping $4,000,000. And now the rest of the story: the consultants' attorney tells the performer that these two dirt-bags have no assets. "You'll be lucky to get five cents on the dollar." As if that were not enough to make this five-year struggle a hollow victory, many agents tell the performer that he will find it hard to get work because he is "too much of a controversial figure." Did this guy win or lose?

In Rossini's opera *The Barber of Seville,* the aging Dr. Bartolo wants to marry his ward, the beautiful and young Rosina. Rosina however, is in love with the dashing Count Almaviva. In order to get the Count out of the picture, Dr. Bartolo makes an unholy alliance with the village priest to "scandalize the Count." In his aria, the priest describes how he will hurt the count "without striking a blow." My translation (from the Italian) is not word for word but paraphrased:

Epilogue

Gossip is like a pebble in a shoe, well-placed it can annoy a giant. If you gather several pebbles you can make a stone. Many stones grow into rocks, then boulders able to crush all that lies in the way.

Gossip is like the ocean rolling up gently to meet the sand. A little wind a light breeze can cause a wave. As the wind begins to intensify, the little wave becomes a breaker and then a giant wave, growing louder and more thunderous until its sound is deafening.

Gossip is a crime for which there is no punishment. Gossip is a crime that doesn't dirty your hands. Gossip is a whisper of words that can destroy.

MALLON PUBLISHING, INC
2637 EAST ATLANTIC BLVD.
#292
POMPANO BEACH, FL
33062-